# FILING AND COMPUTER DATABASE PROJECTS

SECOND EDITION

Jeffrey R. Stewart

Nancy M. Melesco

 Glencoe
McGraw-Hill

New York, New York    Columbus, Ohio    Woodland Hills, California    Peoria, Illinois

*Glencoe/McGraw-Hill*

*A Division of The* **McGraw·Hill** *Companies*

Filing and Computer Database Projects

Copyright © 2002 by The McGraw-Hill Companies, Inc. All rights reserved. Except as permitted under the United States Copyright Act, no part of this publication may be reproduced or distributed in any form or by any means, or stored in a database retrieval system, without the prior written permission of the publisher.

Send all inquiries to:
Glencoe/McGraw-Hill
21600 Oxnard Street, Suite 500
Woodland Hills, CA 91367

ISBN 0-07-822781-X

Printed in the United States of America

5 6 7 8 9 10 073 05

# CONTENTS

**FANFILE**

# FILING AND COMPUTER DATABASE PROJECTS

## Introduction

The five projects in this practice set give you an opportunity to work with both manual files and computer databases. Projects One and Two deal with card filing and correspondence filing. In these projects you will practice indexing, alphabetizing, filing, decision making, and correspondence management. Projects Three, Four, and Five involve the use of the data disk and an electronic database to manage records electronically. In these projects, you will work with a customer database, an inventory database, and an employee database.

## Filing Projects

In Projects One and Two of this practice set, you will work to develop the following competencies:

1. Using a simulated card file, you will file records alphabetically according to the rules for alphabetic filing. These rules, with application practice, appear in Chapter 5 of the textbook *Professional Records and Information Management,* Second Edition, and in Chapter 5 of the textbook *Professional Records Management.* The rules also appear in this workbook beginning on page 23.

2. Using a simulated card file, you will file records by number, by geographic location, and by subject.

3. Using items of correspondence, you will make decisions about which items to file and what further action to take. You will organize these records alphabetically and by subject. You will also practice cross-referencing selected items of correspondence.

Each of the twelve numbered assignments in the filing projects is designed to be completed in approximately one hour. Project One (Assignments 1–8) includes alphabetic, numeric, geographic, and subject card filing. Project Two (Assignments 9A–12) includes alphabetic and subject correspondence filing.

# Card Filing

## Assignment 1: Alphabetic Filing of Individual Names, Cards 1–32

You are a new employee in the sales office of Jacobsen's Department Store in Spanish Lake, Missouri. Jacobsen's is a successful, locally owned business with one large store. Your responsibilities include filing customer names alphabetically according to filing rules 1 through 5.

For this assignment, you will use cards that have the numbers 1 through 32 in the upper right corner. These numbers are for *identification only*—they are not part of the records. You will also use **FanFile,** which is a cardboard sheet that can be folded to form a desk file and thus make it easier to do your work.

Read each step carefully, and complete each step before you continue to the next one.

1.  *Set up FanFile.* Remove FanFile from this workbook, and fold it along the scores so it looks like Figure 1.

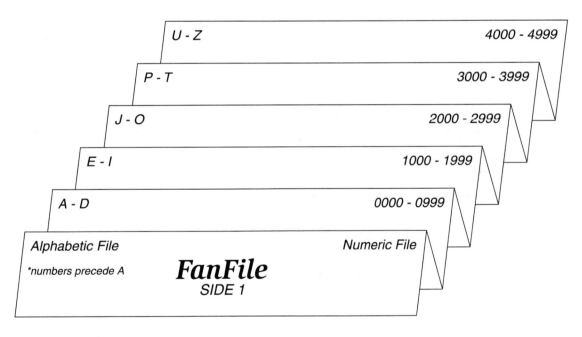

**Figure 1    FanFile folded, side 1**

Place FanFile in front of you so that side 1 is facing you as shown, in Figure 1. Note that there are five pockets in FanFile. Each pocket has a caption at the left for alphabetic filing: A–D, E–I, J–O, P–T, and U–Z. The caption *A–D* means that names having first units beginning with *A, B, C,* or *D* are filed under that caption. The other four captions have the same meaning for their range of letters. For this assignment, you will file the cards in alphabetic order in the five pockets.

2.  *Detach sheets with cards 1–32.* Remove the two sheets from the materials section of this workbook (see Materials for Filing Projects). These sheets have cards with the numbers 1 through 32 in the upper right corners. Do not separate the individual cards yet.

3. *Review.* If you are familiar with filing rules 1 through 5, proceed to the next step. If not, review rules 1 through 5 in your textbook (Chapter 5) or on pages 23–26 of this workbook. You may also review the filing rules by working through the Filing Rules Tutorial disk that is attached to the inside back cover of *Professional Records and Information Management,* Second Edition.

4. *Organize your materials.* Place the two sheets that you removed from this workbook in front of you. Card numbers 1 through 16 on the first sheet and cards 17 through 32 on the second sheet should be facing up. (Ignore the cards on the backs of the two sheets; they will be used in Assignment 2.)

5. *Index.* Index each of the 32 names by writing the names in indexed order on the line above each name. The first name has been indexed for you as an example. Remember to omit any punctuation.

6. *Separate the 32 cards at the perforations.* Arrange them in order from 1 through 32.

7. *File alphabetically.* File each card in correct alphabetic order in the appropriate pocket of FanFile. File each card to the right of its caption so the caption remains visible. For example, card 1 is indexed Zoller Linda J; therefore, card 1 is filed in the U–Z pocket to the right of the U–Z caption, as shown in Figure 2.

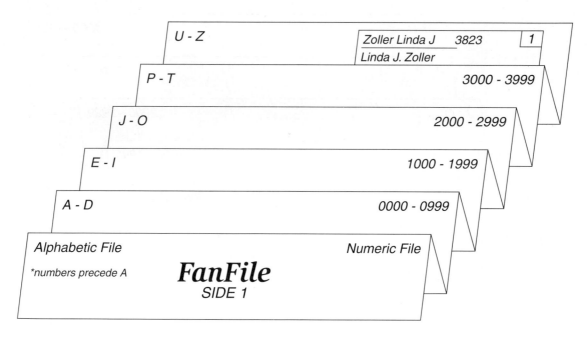

**Figure 2  FanFile with card 1 in right side of pocket U–Z**

Card 2 is indexed Ward Kris D; therefore, card 2 is filed in the U–Z pocket **in front of card 1,** because W comes before Z in the alphabet.

8. *Report your answers.* After all 32 cards have been filed, remove the answer sheet for Assignment 1 from the materials section. Write your name and the date on the answer sheet. Beside each caption on the answer sheet, list the numbers of the cards in the order in which they are arranged in the pocket. Write the card number that is in the box at the upper right corner of each card (not the four-digit number that also appears on each card). As an example, all the numbers for the A–D caption are listed on the answer sheet for you. Be sure that your answers are the same as the example.

9. *Conclude Assignment 1.* Hand in the answer sheet to your instructor. Remove the 32 cards from the five pockets of FanFile. Store them in an envelope until they are used again in Assignment 2.

## Assignment 2: Additional Alphabetic Filing of Individual Names, Cards 33–64

1. *Assemble your materials.* Retrieve the 32 cards used in Assignment 1. Numbers 33 through 64 are on the back (shaded side) of these 32 cards. Arrange these cards in order from 33 through 64.

2. *Set up FanFile.* Place FanFile in front of you so that side 1 is facing you.

3. *Index.* Index each of the 32 names by writing the names in indexed order on the line above each name.

4. *File alphabetically.* File each card in alphabetic order in the appropriate pocket of FanFile. File each card to the right of its caption.

5. *Report your answers.* After all 32 cards have been filed, remove the answer sheet for Assignment 2 from the materials section. Write your name and the date on the answer sheet. Beside each caption on the answer sheet, list the numbers of the cards in the order in which they are arranged in the pocket. Report the card number that appears in the box in the upper right corner of each card.

6. *Conclude Assignment 2.* Hand in the answer sheet to your instructor. Remove the 32 cards from the pockets in FanFile. Store them until they are used again in Assignments 3A and 3B.

## Assignment 3A: Numeric Filing, Cards 1–32

Jacobsen's Department Store keeps a separate numeric card file on all credit customers. The numeric card file is organized according to the four-digit customer numbers. It serves as a reference when the customer number is known but the customer name is not. In this assignment you will practice *numeric* filing with cards 1–32. Follow these instructions:

1. *Assemble your materials.* Retrieve the 32 cards used in Assignments 1 and 2. Using the number in the upper right corner of each card, arrange them in order from 1 through 32.

2. *Set up FanFile.* Place FanFile in front of you so that Side 1 is facing you. Note that each pocket has a numeric caption at the right for numeric filing: 0000–0999, 1000–1999, 2000–2999, 3000–3999, and 4000–4999. The caption *0000–0999* means that numbers from 0000 through 0999 are filed in numeric order under that caption. The other four captions have the same meaning for their range of numbers. For this assignment, you will file the cards in numeric order in each of the five pockets.

3. *Do a rough numeric sort.* Sort the 32 cards into five stacks according to the first digit of the four-digit account number. You will have stacks for 0, 1, 2, 3, and 4.

4. *File numerically.* Working with one stack at a time, file each card in numeric order in the appropriate pocket of FanFile. File each card to the left of the caption so the caption remains visible. For example, card 3 with customer number 0793 is filed in the 0000–0999 pocket to the left of the 0000–0999 caption, as shown in Figure 3.

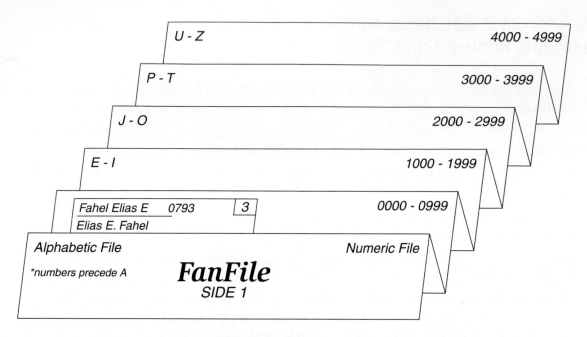

**Figure 3    FanFile with card 3 in left side of pocket 0000–0999**

Card 2 with customer number 0891 is also filed in the 0000–0999 pocket **behind** card 3, because 0891 comes after 0793.

5. *Report your answers.* After all 32 cards have been filed, remove the answer sheet for Assignment 3A from the materials section. Write your name and the date on the answer sheet. Beside each caption on the answer sheet, list the numbers of the cards in the order in which they are arranged in the pocket. Report the card number that is in the box at the upper right corner of each card, not the four-digit customer number. As an example, all of the numbers for the 0000–0999 caption are listed on the answer sheet for you. Be sure that your answers are the same as the example.

6. *Conclude Assignment 3A.* Hand in the answer sheet to your instructor. Remove the 32 cards from the five pockets in FanFile. Store them until they are used again in Assignment 3B.

## Assignment 3B: Additional Numeric Filing, Cards 33–64

1. *Assemble your materials.* Retrieve the 32 cards used in Assignment 3A. Numbers 33 through 64 are on the back of these 32 cards. Arrange these cards in order from 33 through 64.

2. *Set up FanFile.* Place FanFile in front of you so that side 1 is facing you. For this assignment, use cards 33 through 64 and the answer sheet for Assignment 3B.

3. *Do a rough numeric sort.* Sort the 32 cards into five stacks according to the first digit of the four-digit account number. You will have stacks for 0, 1, 2, 3, and 4.

4. *File numerically.* Working with one stack at a time, file each card in numeric order in the appropriate pocket of FanFile. File each card to the left of the caption so the caption remains visible.

5. *Report your answers.* After all 32 cards have been filed, remove the answer sheet for Assignment 3B from the materials section. Fill in your name and the date. Beside each caption on the answer sheet, list the numbers of the cards in the order in which they are arranged in the pocket. Report the card number that is in the box at the upper right corner of each card.

6. *Conclude Assignment 3B.* Hand in the answer sheet to your instructor. Remove the 32 cards from the five pockets in FanFile. With your instructor's consent, discard them or deposit them for recycling.

This assignment concludes your manual filing practice with Jacobsen's Department Store. You will do electronic filing for Jacobsen's in Project Three.

## Assignment 4: Alphabetic Filing of Business and Organization Names, Cards 65–96

You have secured a position as a new employee in the offices of Fidelity Underwriters, Inc. in Los Angeles, California. Your new employer handles the employee group insurance plans for several businesses, organizations, and government agencies. Fidelity's clients are located in five geographic regions of the United States. Your first assignment is to file client records alphabetically according to filing rules 6 through 12.

For this assignment, you will use cards that have the numbers 65 through 96 in the upper right corner. Follow these steps:

1. *Set up FanFile.* Place FanFile in front of you so that side 1 is facing you. For this assignment you will use the alphabetic captions at the left as you did in Assignments 1 and 2.

2. *Detach sheets with cards 65–96.* Remove the two sheets from the materials section of this workbook that have cards with the numbers 65 through 96 in the upper right corner. Do not separate the individual cards yet.

3. *Review.* If you are familiar with filing rules 6 through 12, proceed to the next step. If not, review filing rules 6 through 12 in your textbook (Chapter 5) or on pages 26–30 of this workbook. You may also review the filing rules by completing the Filing Rules Tutorial that is on the disk inside the back cover of *Professional Records and Information Management,* Second Edition.

4. *Organize your materials.* Place the two sheets that you removed from this workbook in front of you. Card numbers 65 through 80 on the first sheet and cards 81 through 96 on the second sheet should be facing up. Ignore the cards on the backs of the two sheets. They will be used in Assignment 5.

5. *Index.* Index each of the 32 names by writing the names in indexed order on the line above each name. The first name has been indexed for you as an example. Remember to omit any punctuation.

6. *Separate the 32 cards at the perforations.* Arrange these cards in order from 65 through 96.

7. *File alphabetically.* File each card in alphabetic order in the appropriate pocket of FanFile. If the first indexed unit on a card is an Arabic number, such as 4, file the card in numeric order in the A–D pocket before names beginning with A. File each card to the right of its caption. Use the same procedures followed in Assignments 1 and 2.

8. *Report your answers.* After all 32 cards have been filed, remove the answer sheet for Assignment 4 from this workbook. Write your name and the date on the answer sheet. Beside each caption on the answer sheet, list the numbers of the cards in the order in which they are arranged in the pocket.

9. *Conclude Assignment 4.* Hand in the answer sheet to your instructor. Remove the 32 cards from the five pockets of FanFile. Store them until they are used again in Assignment 5.

## Assignment 5: Additional Alphabetic Filing of Business and Organization Names, Cards 97–128

1. *Assemble your materials.* Retrieve the 32 cards used in Assignment 4. Numbers 97 through 128 appear on the back of these 32 cards. Arrange these cards in order from 97 through 128.

2. *Set up FanFile.* Place FanFile in front of you so that side 1 is facing you. Use the alphabetic captions.

3. *Index.* Index each of the 32 names as you did in Assignment 4.

4. *File alphabetically.* File each card in alphabetic order in the appropriate pocket of FanFile. File each card to the right of its caption.

5. *Report your answers.* After all 32 cards have been filed, remove the answer sheet for Assignment 5. Fill in your name and the date. Beside each caption list the numbers of the cards in the order in which they are arranged in the pocket.

6. *Conclude Assignment 5.* Hand in the answer sheet to your instructor. Remove the 32 cards from the pockets of FanFile. Store them until they are used again in Assignments 6A and 6B.

## Assignment 6A: Geographic Filing, Cards 65–96

Fidelity Underwriters, Inc. keeps a separate geographic card file on all clients. The geographic card file is organized according to five geographic regions of the United States. The geographic card file is helpful in generating mailings and other activities conducted by each region. In this assignment, you will practice geographic filing with cards 65 through 96. Follow these instructions:

1. *Assemble your materials.* Retrieve the 32 cards used in Assignments 4 and 5. Arrange these cards in order from 65 through 96.

2. *Set up FanFile.* Place FanFile in front of you so that side 2 is facing you. Note that each pocket has a geographic caption at the right for geographic filing: NC (North Central)

Region, NE (Northeast) Region, NW (Northwest) Region, SC (South Central) Region, and SE (Southeast) Region. You will file the cards for this assignment in geographic order in the five pockets.

3. *Do a rough geographic sort.* Sort the 32 cards into five stacks according to region. On each card, a two-letter regional abbreviation is located to the right of the line. You will have stacks for NC, NE, NW, SC, and SE.

4. *File geographically.* Working with one stack at a time, file each card in geographic order in the appropriate pocket of FanFile. Within each region, file the cards alphabetically by the two-letter state abbreviation as the abbreviation is written. If both the region and the state are the same, file cards alphabetically by the name of the city. If region, state, and city are the same, file cards alphabetically by business or organization name. For example, cards 65, 75, and 96 are all filed in the NC (North Central) Region to the left of the caption. Card 75 (IA) is filed **in front of** card 96 (IL) because *A* comes before *L*. Card 96 is filed **in front of** card 65 (NE) because *I* comes before *N*.

5. *Report your answers.* After all 32 cards have been filed, remove the answer sheet for Assignment 6A. Fill in your name and the date. Beside each caption on the answer sheet, list the numbers of the cards in the order in which they are arranged in the pocket. Report the card number that is in the box at the upper right corner of each card. As an example, the first number for the NC Region caption is listed on the answer sheet for you.

6. *Conclude Assignment 6A.* Hand in the answer sheet to your instructor. Remove the 32 cards from the pockets of FanFile. Store them until they are used again in Assignment 6B.

## Assignment 6B: Geographic Filing, Cards 97–128

1. *Assemble your materials.* Retrieve the 32 cards used in Assignment 6A. Arrange these cards in order from 97 through 128.

2. *Set up FanFile.* Place FanFile so that side 2 faces you. For this assignment, use cards 97 through 128 and the answer sheet for Assignment 6B.

3. *Do a rough geographic sort.* Sort the 32 cards into five stacks according to region.

4. *File geographically.* Working with one stack at a time, file each card in geographic order in the appropriate pocket of FanFile. Within each region, file the cards alphabetically by the two-letter state abbreviation.

5. *Report your answers.* After all 32 cards have been filed, remove the answer sheet for Assignment 6B. Fill in your name and the date. Beside each caption on the answer sheet, list the numbers of the cards in the order in which they are arranged in the pocket.

6. *Conclude Assignment 6B.* Hand in the answer sheet to your instructor. Remove the 32 cards from the pockets of FanFile. With your instructor's consent, discard them or deposit them for recycling.

This assignment concludes your manual filing practice with Fidelity Underwriters, Inc.

# Assignment 7A: Subject Filing, Cards 129–160

You have been hired to manage the inventory records at New Age Office Supply. The company is a retail business that sells five basic categories of office furniture, equipment, and supplies. Because inventory records refer to items rather than people or businesses, you will file the inventory records by subject. In the subject system used by New Age, a product code is assigned to every type of product in inventory. The product code begins with a letter of the alphabet—A, B, C, D, and E—for each of the five major product lines. The rest of the product code is numeric. A typical product code looks like this: E1-0245.

For this assignment, you will use cards that have the numbers 129 through 160 in the upper right corner. Follow these steps:

1. *Set up FanFile.* Place FanFile in front of you so that side 2 is facing you. For this assignment you will use the subject captions on the left side of the pocket. These subject captions identify each of New Age's major product lines: A—Furniture, B—File Cabinets, C—Accessories, D—Visible Files, and E—Carriers. For this assignment, you will sort the cards into product lines by using the first *letter* of the product code. Then, within each product line, you will file the cards in numeric order using the *numbers* of the product code.

2. *Detach sheets with cards 129–160.* Remove the two sheets from the materials section of this workbook that have cards with the numbers 129 through 160 in the upper right corner.

3. *Separate the 32 cards at the perforations.*

4. *Do a rough sort.* Sort the 32 cards into five stacks according to the letter at the beginning of each product code. You will have stacks for A, B, C, D, and E.

5. *File by product code.* Working with one stack at a time, file each card in numeric order in the appropriate pocket of FanFile. File each card to the right of its caption. Within a pocket, file cards in numeric order using the five digits in the product code. Ignore the hyphen in the product number. For example, card 136 with product code D1-0284 is filed in the D—Visible Files pocket **in front of** card 132 because D1-0284 comes before D1-0333. Card 147 with product code D1-0425 is filed in front of card 156 (D2-0147) because D1 comes before D2.

6. *Report your answers.* After all 32 cards have been filed, remove the answer sheet for Assignment 7A. Fill in your name and the date. Beside each caption list the numbers of the cards in the order in which they are arranged in the pocket.

7. *Conclude Assignment 7A.* Hand in the answer sheet to your instructor. Remove the 32 cards from the pockets in FanFile. Store them until they are used again in Assignment 7B.

# Assignment 7B: Subject Filing, Cards 161–192

1. *Assemble your materials.* Retrieve the 32 cards used in Assignment 7A. Numbers 161 through 192 appear on the back of these 32 cards. Arrange the cards in order from 161 through 192.

2. *Set up FanFile.* Place FanFile in front of you so that side 2 faces you.

3. *Do a rough sort.* Sort the 32 cards into five stacks according to the letter at the beginning of each product code.

4. *File by product code.* Working with only one stack at a time, file each card in numeric order in the appropriate pocket of FanFile. File each card to the right of its caption.

5. *Report your answers.* After all 32 cards have been filed, remove the answer sheet for Assignment 7B. Fill in your name and the date. Beside each caption list the numbers of the cards in the order in which they are arranged in the pocket.

6. *Conclude Assignment 7B.* Hand in the answer sheet to your instructor. Remove the 32 cards from the pockets of FanFile. With your instructor's consent, discard them or deposit them for recycling.

This assignment concludes your manual filing practice with New Age Office Supplies. You will do electronic filing for New Age in Project Four.

## Assignment 8: Project Quiz

Your instructor will give you the Project Quiz for Project One—Card Filing. Use the answer sheet for Assignment 8 to record your answers to the Project Quiz.

# Alphabetic and Subject Correspondence Filing

You have been hired by Scorcher Athletics, Inc. as their filing administrator. Your main responsibility is to manage hard copy incoming and outgoing correspondence (e-mail is managed by another worker). You are a new employee, so the following information is part of your orientation to the company.

Scorcher Athletics, Inc. is located in Boston, Massachusetts. It produces sportswear and athletic shoes. Scorcher buys leather materials from Regal Leathers in Boston. Scorcher also buys nylon fabric materials and some sportswear designs from Tough-Tear Nylon Company in Cambridge, Massachusetts. Scorcher has a contract with Reggie's Trucking Company in Boston. Reggie's delivers the materials that Scorcher buys to one of its fabricating contractors, Sportswear Sewing Center. The people at Sportswear sew or assemble the materials according to Scorcher's designs. After the products are constructed, several retail stores, such as Sports & Weights Unlimited in Cambridge, purchase the new stock to sell to consumers.

In the past few months, Scorcher has been developing a new running shoe design. It has been supported enthusiastically by the president of the company, Ahmal Jackson. The new design was formally approved by Scorcher in early July (last month). Roxanne Knight is Scorcher's vice president for production, and she is in charge of implementing the manufacturing of the new line of running shoes.

Regal Leathers has been conducting leather treatment tests to develop chemicals that are more environmentally sound than those they use now, and they have been successful. The new chemical treatment, which actually improves the characteristics of the leather, received federal approval on July 25. The people at Regal Leathers believe Scorcher should try the new leather treatment on its new running shoes. Regal suggests that Scorcher introduce this new product as the *Envirun* shoe. Regal Leathers will produce the new treated leather at their Milford facility instead of their Newton plant, a move that will require some rerouting for the trucking services.

Meanwhile, Tough-Tear Nylon Company has developed a new line of sportswear that coordinates with the design of Scorcher's new *Envirun* shoe. One of Scorcher's best customers, Sports & Weights Unlimited, has begun to prepare its store for this *Envirun* line of sportswear.

# Assignment 9A: Managing Incoming and Outgoing Correspondence, Items 1–12

In Assignments 9A through 11, you will manage 24 items of correspondence for Scorcher Athletics, Inc. Some of these items of correspondence are incoming; others are outgoing. Each item of correspondence has a number in its upper right corner. This number is for identification purposes only and is not part of the records.

For Assignment 9A, you will deal with the first 12 items of correspondence. You will screen each item, decide what action to take, and then file it according to the name of the business to which it was sent or from which it was received.

1. *Detach and examine sheets containing correspondence items 1–12.* Remove correspondence items 1 through 12 from the materials section of this workbook (see Materials for Filing Projects). Correspondence on the Scorcher Athletics, Inc. letterhead is a copy of outgoing correspondence. Correspondence on all other letterheads is incoming—either an original copy or a faxed copy.

2. *Separate the 12 items of correspondence at the perforations.* Beginning with the correspondence identified as number 1, arrange the correspondence in numeric order.

3. *Detach and examine the answer sheet.* Remove the answer sheet for Assignment 9A. Fill in your name and the date. Notice the headings on the answer sheet: Item No., Discard? (Yes or No), Alphabetic Caption, and Action.

4. *Screen the correspondence.* Look at each item of correspondence to determine whether it should be kept or discarded according to the following guidelines:

   a. Outgoing correspondence—all copies of outgoing correspondence, that is, correspondence on Scorcher letterhead, should be kept. The fact that a copy was made means that it was important enough to be kept and filed. Therefore, write an X under No in the Discard? column of your answer sheet. Place the item face down in a stack of correspondence to be kept.

   b. Incoming correspondence—If incoming correspondence is important to the operations of the business, it should be kept; if it is not, then it should be discarded. Correspondence that relates to accounts payable or accounts receivable, marketing and advertising, shipping and transportation, and designs or specifications of products is important to the operations of the business and should be kept. Therefore, write an X under No in the Discard? column of your answer sheet. Place the item on the stack for correspondence to be kept.

      Correspondence about unsolicited merchandise and credit services and routine announcements about business closings and employees should not be kept. Therefore, write an X under Yes in the Discard? column of your answer sheet. Place the items in a stack for correspondence to be discarded.

   c. After screening the 12 items, check to be sure that an X has been written under either Yes or No in the Discard? column of your answer sheet for all 12 items.

   d. Put the items to be discarded inside the back cover of this workbook. Do not throw away these items until you are instructed to do so.

   e. Place the stack of items to be kept in front of you. The lowest numbered item should be on top.

5. *Determine the alphabetic caption.* All items of correspondence will be filed by a business name.

   a. Select the caption under which each item of correspondence will be filed.

      **(1)** Incoming correspondence—use the business name in the letterhead.

      **(2)** Outgoing correspondence—use the business name that appears in the inside address. Do not use the name of the employee who is sending or receiving the item.

   b. Draw a line under the complete name of the business chosen as the caption under which the correspondence will be filed.

   c. On the answer sheet, write the name of the business chosen for the alphabetic filing caption. The first caption has been entered for you on the answer sheet as an example. For discarded items, no alphabetic caption should be entered on the answer sheet.

   d. After completing all the items in the stack, check to be sure that an alphabetic caption has been written on the answer sheet for all items except those to be discarded.

6. *Process the correspondence.* Read each item of correspondence to be kept. Determine what action is to be taken with the item. Write the action at the upper left corner of the correspondence and in the Action column of the answer sheet. Some items of correspondence will have more than one action. Action choices are listed below.

   a. *File:* The action for all copies of outgoing correspondence is *File.*

   b. *Route to president:* The action for any incoming items addressed to Ahmal Jackson is *Route to president.*

   c. *Route to vice president:* The action for any incoming items addressed to Roxanne Knight is *Route to vice president.*

   d. *Cross-reference:* The action for any item to be cross-referenced is *Cross-reference.* For your practice, only items 8 and 21 will be cross-referenced although it is possible that in an actual situation, others also would be cross-referenced. On item 8, draw a line under Regal Leathers in the body of the letter and write an *X* to the right of the end of the line. The *X* indicates that the underlined name will be a cross-reference caption. Write *File and cross-reference* in the upper left corner of the letter and in the Action column of the answer sheet. Remove a cross-reference sheet from the materials section of this workbook. Fill in the cross-reference sheet as follows:

      • Beside Name at the top of the sheet, write *Regal Leathers.*

      • Beside File No. at the top of the sheet, write *8X.*

      • Beside Regarding, write *Transporting new products.*

      • Beside Date, write the date of the item, *8/8/—.*

      • Beside Name under SEE (on the lower part of the sheet), write *Reggie's Trucking Company.*

      • Beside File No. on the lower part of the sheet, write the item number, *8.*

      • Place the cross-reference sheet with your stack of correspondence.

7. *Conclude Assignment 9A.* Hand in the answer sheet to your instructor. Store the items of correspondence until they are used again in Assignments 10 and 11.

## Assignment 9B: Managing Incoming and Outgoing Correspondence, Items 13–24

1. *Detach sheets containing correspondence items 13–24.* Remove correspondence items 13 through 24 from the materials section of this workbook (see Materials for Filing Projects).

2. *Separate the 12 items of correspondence at the perforations.* Beginning with item 13, arrange the correspondence in numeric order.

3. *Detach the answer sheet.* Remove the answer sheet for Assignment 9B. Fill in your name and the date.

4. *Screen the correspondence as you did in Assignment 9A (step 4).*

5. *Determine the alphabetic caption of the correspondence you decided to keep.* Then follow the procedures in Assignment 9A, step 5.

6. *Process the correspondence.* Process the correspondence as you did for Assignment 9A (step 6). For item 21, prepare a cross-reference sheet. The cross-reference caption is Regal Leathers. In the Action column of your answer sheet and in the upper left corner of item 21, write *Route to vice president, cross-reference,* and *file.*

7. *Conclude Assignment 9B.* Hand in the answer sheet to your instructor. Store the items of correspondence until they are used again in Assignments 10 and 11.

## Assignment 10: Alphabetic Filing of Correspondence

In this assignment, you will simulate the filing of the items of correspondence used in Assignments 9A and 9B. You may assume that they have been received and are ready to be filed. Before you begin, check to see that you have indicated on the answer sheet the correct items to be discarded. Items that should have been marked to be discarded are numbers 3 and 4 in Assignment 9A and numbers 22 and 23 in Assignment 9B. For this assignment, you will use the 20 items other than the four that should have been discarded. You will also use the two cross-reference sheets prepared in Assignments 9A and 9B. Follow these steps in simulating the filing of the 20 items and two cross-reference sheets:

1. *Organize your materials.* Arrange the 20 items of correspondence in numerical order according to the identification number in the upper right corner. Place the items in front of you, with the lowest numbered item at the top. Cross-reference sheets 8X and 21X follow items 8 and 21, respectively.

2. *Sort alphabetically.* Sort the items into separate stacks according to the name of the company that was underscored in Assignment 9A or 9B. For example, you will have a stack for Regal Leathers and other stacks for the other companies. For the cross-reference sheets, the filing caption is the name at the top of the sheet.

3. *Arrange chronologically.* Arrange each of the stacks by date, or chronologically. Correspondence is filed in folders with the most recent date in front. Thus, each stack should have the most recent item on top and the oldest item on the bottom.

4. *Detach the answer sheet.* Remove the answer sheet for Assignment 10. Fill in your name and the date.

5. *File alphabetically.* Simulate filing the items by writing the number of each item beside its caption on the answer sheet. The first item has been recorded on the answer sheet as an example. For each caption, be sure that the number for the item with the most recent date is listed first. That number should be followed by the numbers of other items in chronological order from the most recent to the oldest. Report the cross-reference sheets as numbers 8X and 21X.

6. *Conclude Assignment 10.* Hand in the answer sheet to your instructor. Discard the two cross-reference sheets. Store the items of correspondence until they are used again in Assignment 11.

## Assignment 11: Subject Filing of Correspondence

In this assignment, you will simulate the filing of the items of correspondence used in Assignment 10. This time you will file the items by subject. For this assignment, you will use only the 20 items that were kept. Follow these steps in simulating the filing of the 20 items by subject.

1. *Organize your materials.* Arrange the items of correspondence in numerical order according to the identification number in the upper right corner. Place the items in front of you with the lowest numbered item on top.

2. *Code by subject.* Read each item of correspondence and determine which of the following subject captions best fits the topic of that correspondence. Write the subject caption in the upper right corner of the item. Subject caption choices are listed below.

   a. *Accounts payable:* This subject caption is for items related to amounts owed by Scorcher to its suppliers.

   b. *Accounts receivable:* This subject caption is for items related to amounts owed to Scorcher by its customers.

   c. *Marketing and Advertising:* This subject caption is for items dealing with the sale and promotion of Scorcher products.

   d. *Specifications:* This subject caption is for items having to do with manufacturing requirements, materials, and designs for Scorcher products.

   e. *Transportation:* This subject caption is for items related to shipping, routes, and delivery of products to or from Scorcher and its contractors.

3. *Sort by subject.* Sort the items into separate stacks according to the subject filing captions that were written in step 2. You will have five stacks—one for each of the subject captions listed above.

4. *Arrange chronologically.* Arrange each of the stacks by date, or chronologically. Correspondence filed by subject at Scorcher Athletics is organized in folders, with the

most recent date in front. So each stack should have the most recent item on top and the oldest item on the bottom. Do not arrange the items alphabetically by business name.

5. *Detach the answer sheet.* Remove the answer sheet for Assignment 11. Fill in your name and the date.

6. *File by subject.* Simulate filing the items by writing the number of each item beside its caption on the answer sheet. The first item has been recorded on the answer sheet as an example. For each subject caption, be sure that the number for the item with the most recent date is listed first. That number should be followed by the numbers of other items in chronological order, from the most recent to the oldest.

7. *Conclude Assignment 11.* Hand in the answer sheet and correspondence items 20 and 21 to your instructor. Items 20 and 21 will be used in Assignment 12, Project Quiz. With your instructor's consent, discard or deposit for recycling all of the other items of correspondence.

## Assignment 12: Project Quiz

Your instructor will give you correspondence items 20 and 21 and the quiz for Project Two—Alphabetic and Subject Correspondence Filing.

# RULES FOR ALPHABETIC FILING

The twelve rules for alphabetic filing on the following pages are compatible with those adopted by ARMA International. To interpret the rules correctly, you must be able to use four special terms related to alphabetic filing.

**Unit.** Each part of a name is a unit. The name *Teronda Jean Clark* has three units: *Teronda, Jean,* and *Clark.* The name *National Rollerblade Manufacturing Company* has four units; *The North Carolina Computer Institute* has five units.

**Indexing.** Indexing is determining the order and format of the units in a name when alphabetizing. To index names, we must know the answer to questions such as these: Is a person's record filed by the first or last name? Is a business record filed under *T* if the name begins with *The?* Is punctuation considered in alphabetizing a name? You will learn the answers to these and other questions about indexing as you study the twelve rules.

**Alphabetizing.** When you arrange names in alphabetic order, you are alphabetizing them. The names *Bolling, Chou,* and *Diez* are arranged in alphabetic order because *B* comes before *C,* and *C* comes before *D.* The names *Jackson, Jefferson,* and *Jonas* are also arranged in alphabetic order. They each begin with J but the second letter is different. These second letters are in correct alphabetic order; *a* comes before *e* and *e* comes before *o.*

**Case.** The case of a letter of the alphabet refers to whether it is written as a capital letter (A), called *uppercase,* or as a small letter *(a),* called *lowercase.* When you alphabetize, it makes no difference whether a letter is written in uppercase or lowercase. Consider an uppercase letter to be identical to its lowercase counterpart. For example, in filing, the name *McArthur* is considered to be exactly the same as *Mcarthur.*

## Alphabetizing Unit by Unit

In the chart below, the names are divided into units.

| Name | Unit 1 | Unit 2 | Unit 3 |
|------|--------|--------|--------|
| Partyshop | Partyshop | | |
| Pettinger Company | Pettinger | Company | |
| Pettinger Manufacturers | Pettinger | Manufacturers | |
| Rawls Communications | Rawls | Communications | |
| Rawls Dynasty Computers | Rawls | Dynasty | Computers |
| Rawls Dynasty Diner | Rawls | Dynasty | Diner |

The first step in alphabetizing unit by unit is to alphabetize first units. Note the following about the above chart:

1. The names under Unit 1 are in alphabetic order.

2. The name *Pettinger* appears twice in the Unit 1 column. If first units are the same, alphabetize second units. In the chart above, note that the names beside *Pettinger* under Unit 2, *Company* and *Manufacturers,* are in alphabetic order.

**3.** The name *Rawls* appears three times in the Unit 1 column. If first *and* second units are the same, alphabetize third units. In the chart above, note that the third units, *Computers* and *Diner,* determine the alphabetic order of the last two names.

**Nothing Comes Before Something.** In alphabetizing, an important guideline to remember is *nothing comes before something.* A name such as *Park* comes before a name such as *Parke.* Another example is shown in the chart below.

| Name | Unit 1 | Unit 2 |
|---|---|---|
| Kiddytoys | Kiddytoys | |
| Kiddytoys Circus | Kiddytoys | Circus |

Note that *Kiddytoys* comes before *Kiddytoys Circus* because nothing comes before something *(Circus).* A third example of the *nothing-comes-before-something* principle is shown below.

| Name | Unit 1 | Unit 2 | Unit 3 |
|---|---|---|---|
| Millford Rest Stop | Millford | Rest | Stop |
| Millford Restaurant | Millford | Restaurant | |

In the example above, *Millford Rest Stop* comes before *Millford Restaurant* because *Rest* comes before *Restaurant.*

# Twelve Filing Rules

### Rule 1: Names of Individuals

When indexing the name of a person, arrange the parts of the name in this order: last name as unit 1, first name or initial as unit 2, and middle name or initial as unit 3.

| Name | Unit 1 | Unit 2 | Unit 3 |
|---|---|---|---|
| S. D. Abrams | Abrams | S | D |
| Jim Bolen | Bolen | Jim | |
| Jim R. Bolen | Bolen | Jim | R |
| Anne R. Cirillo | Cirillo | Anne | R |
| B. Tina Cirillo | Cirillo | B | Tina |
| Beverly Maria Cirillo | Cirillo | Beverly | Maria |

### Rule 2: Personal Names with Prefixes

Consider a prefix, such as Mc in McDonald, as part of the name it precedes. Ignore any apostrophe or space that appears within or after the prefix. Commonly used prefixes are d', D', de, De, Del, De la, Di, Du, El, Fitz, La, Le, M, Mac, Mc, O', Saint, St., Van, Van de, Van der, Von, and Von der.

| Name | Unit 1 | Unit 2 | Unit 3 |
|------|--------|--------|--------|
| Floyd K. D'Atre | DAtre | Floyd | K |
| Emma J. De Hart | DeHart | Emma | J |
| Flora Dehart | Dehart | Flora | |
| Charles Dean MacDowell | MacDowell | Charles | Dean |
| Charles McDowell | McDowell | Charles | |
| Phillip O'Day | ODay | Phillip | |
| Linda Saint John | SaintJohn | Linda | |
| Charlotte L. St.Jean | StJean | Charlotte | L |
| Ashley VanAllen | VanAllen | Ashley | |
| Jenah A. Van Balen | VanBalen | Jenah | A |

## Rule 3: Hyphenated Personal Names

Consider a hyphenated first, middle, or last name as one unit.

| Name | Unit 1 | Unit 2 | Unit 3 |
|------|--------|--------|--------|
| Willard G. Corvin-Rojas | CorvinRojas | Willard | G |
| Shawn-Lea Czinzack | Czinzack | ShawnLea | |
| Johanna Dejong | Dejong | Johanna | |
| Antonio R. Dejong-Valdez | DejongValdez | Antonio | R |

## Rule 4: Abbreviated Personal Names

Abbreviated and shortened forms of personal names are indexed as written.

| Name | Unit 1 | Unit 2 | Unit 3 |
|------|--------|--------|--------|
| Jos. R. Randolph | Randolph | Jos | R |
| Liz Ritchie | Ritchie | Liz | |
| Billy Dee Rowland | Rowland | Billy | Dee |
| Geo. Catlin Rutland | Rutland | Geo | Catlin |

## Rule 5: Personal Names with Titles and Suffixes

When used with a person's name, a title or a suffix is the last indexing unit. It is used to distinguish between two or more identical names. Titles and suffixes are indexed as written. Titles include Capt., Dr., Mayor, Miss, Mr., Mrs., Ms., and Senator. Suffixes include seniority terms (II, III, Jr., Sr.) and professional designations (CPA, CRM [Certified Records Manager], M.D., Ph.D.).

| Name | Unit 1 | Unit 2 | Unit 3 | Unit 4 |
|------|--------|--------|--------|--------|
| Carol King, CPA | King | Carol | CPA | |
| Dr. Carol King | King | Carol | Dr | |
| Miss Holly W. Lazar | Lazar | Holly | W | Miss |

| Name | Unit 1 | Unit 2 | Unit 3 | Unit 4 |
|------|--------|--------|--------|--------|
| Mrs. Holly W. Lazar | Lazar | Holly | W | Mrs |
| Daryl E. Mabry, II | Mabry | Daryl | E | II |
| Daryl E. Mabry, III | Mabry | Daryl | E | III |
| Daryl E. Mabry, Jr. | Mabry | Daryl | E | Jr |
| Daryl E. Mabry, Sr. | Mabry | Daryl | E | Sr |
| Capt. Lisa R. Martino | Martino | Lisa | R | Capt |
| Lisa R. Martino, CRM | Martino | Lisa | R | CRM |

*Note:* Numeric seniority terms (II, III) are filed before alphabetic terms (Jr. and Sr.)

## Rule 6: Names of Businesses and Organizations

Consider the units in business and organization names in the order in which they are normally written. To determine the order in which a business or organization name is normally written, use the letterhead of the business or organization. If the letterhead is not available, use alternate sources such as directories, advertisements, and computer databases. When *The* is the first word of the name, it is treated as the last unit. Names with prefixes are considered as one unit, just as with personal names.

| Name | Unit 1 | Unit 2 | Unit 3 | Unit 4 |
|------|--------|--------|--------|--------|
| Allegheny Realty | Allegheny | Realty | | |
| Anna Lang Studios | Anna | Lang | Studios | |
| Bank of the Northwest | Bank | of | the | Northwest |
| The Bank of Vermont | Bank | of | Vermont | The |
| C H Detective Agency | C | H | Detective | Agency |
| CCR Car Rentals | CCR | Car | Rentals | |
| Dymock and Weddle | Dymock | and | Weddle | |
| East Coast Fun Park | East | Coast | Fun | Park |
| Eastcoasters Bicycle Company | Eastcoasters | Bicycle | Company | |
| El Toro Industries | ElToro | Industries | | |
| Hospital of Olympia | Hospital | of | Olympia | |
| The Jackson Marketing News | Jackson | Marketing | News | The |
| Marie Scott High School | Marie | Scott | High | School |
| South East Laundromat | South | East | Laundromat | |
| University of Connecticut | University | of | Connecticut | |

## Rule 7: Abbreviations in Business and Organization Names

Abbreviations in business and organization names are indexed as written. Ignore the period at the end of an abbreviation.

| Name | Unit 1 | Unit 2 | Unit 3 | Unit 4 |
|------|--------|--------|--------|--------|
| Carpets Ltd. of PA | Carpets | Ltd | of | PA |
| Data Systems, Inc. | Data | Systems | Inc | |
| Dr. Pepper Bottling Co. | Dr | Pepper | Bottling | Co |
| Lt. Penn Equipment Co. | Lt | Penn | Equipment | Co |
| Ms. Sport Smartwear | Ms | Sport | Smartwear | |
| N. J. Boothe Agy. | N | J | Boothe | Agy |
| Regal Mfg. Corp. | Regal | Mfg | Corp | |

## Rule 8: Punctuation in Business and Organization Names

Ignore any punctuation marks that appear in business and organization names. Hyphenated business and organization names are treated as one unit. Punctuation marks include the apostrophe ('), colon (:), comma (,), dash (—), diagonal slash (/), exclamation point (!), hyphen (-), parentheses ( ), period (.), question mark (?), quotation marks (" "), and semicolon (;).

| Name | Unit 1 | Unit 2 | Unit 3 |
|------|--------|--------|--------|
| "Bob" McFall Farms | Bob | McFall | Farms |
| Cole-Elliott Used Parts | ColeElliott | Used | Parts |
| Economy Rent-a-Car | Economy | RentaCar | |
| For Joy! Tenniswear | For | Joy | Tenniswear |
| How's That? Burgers | Hows | That | Burgers |
| Van's Storage Co. | Vans | Storage | Co |

## Rule 9: Numbers in Business and Organization Names

Arabic numbers (2, 17) are considered one unit and are filed in numeric order before alphabetic characters. Hyphenated numbers (7-11) are indexed according to the number before the hyphen (7); the number after the hyphen (11) is ignored. An arabic number followed by a hyphen and a word (7-Gable) or a hyphen and a letter (4-N-1) is considered one unit (7Gable, 4N1). Thus, names such as 7-11 Store, 4-N-1 Bargain Store, 6-20 Shop, and 4-Seasons Restaurant are indexed and alphabetized as 4N1 Bargain Store, 4Seasons Restaurant, 6 Shop, and 7 Store. If a number in a business or organization name is spelled out (First Street Pizza) it is filed alphabetically as written. Hyphenated numbers that are spelled out (Twenty-One Restaurant) are considered one unit (TwentyOne Restaurant). The letters *st*, *d*, and *th* following an arabic number are ignored. Thus, 1st is indexed as 1, 2nd or 2d as 2, 3rd or 3d as 3, 4th as 4, and so on.

| Name | Unit 1 | Unit 2 | Unit 3 | Unit 4 |
|------|--------|--------|--------|--------|
| 7 Flags Over Texas | 7 | Flags | Over | Texas |
| 7-11 Food Store | 7 | Food | Store | |
| 7th Swan Swimwear Co. | 7 | Swan | Swimwear | Co |

| Name | Unit 1 | Unit 2 | Unit 3 | Unit 4 |
|---|---|---|---|---|
| 11 Pipers Music Shop | 11 | Pipers | Music | Shop |
| 99 Flavors Yogurt Parlor | 99 | Flavors | Yogurt | Parlor |
| 1400 Allendale Apts. | 1400 | Allendale | Apts | |
| Fifty-Fifty Autocar Sales Co. | FiftyFifty | Autocar | Sales | Co |
| Forty Mile Steakhouse | Forty | Mile | Steakhouse | |
| Four Corners Pharmacy | Four | Corners | Pharmacy | |
| Fourth and Main Photography | Fourth | and | Main | Photography |
| Galen's 6-Way Wrench Co. | Galens | 6Way | Wrench | Co |
| Galen's Auction Flea Market | Galens | Auction | Flea | Market |
| Wayco 8 Way Carwash | Wayco | 8 | Way | Carwash |
| The Wayco Eight, Inc. | Wayco | Eight | Inc | The |

## Rule 10: Symbols in Business and Organization Names

If a symbol is part of a name, the symbol is indexed as if spelled out, as shown here:

| Symbol | Indexed As |
|---|---|
| & | and |
| ¢ | cent or cents |
| $ | dollar or dollars |
| # | number or pounds |
| % | percent |

| Name | Unit 1 | Unit 2 | Unit 3 | Unit 4 |
|---|---|---|---|---|
| 58th Street Deli Mart | 58 | Street | Deli | Mart |
| The 58¢ Beef Giant | 58cent | Beef | Giant | The |
| A & R Appliances | A | and | R | Appliances |
| $ Saver Used Books | Dollar | Saver | Used | Books |
| # One Phone Center | Number | One | Phone | Center |

*Note:* When the $ sign is used before a number, file first under the number. For example, $60 Motel is indexed 60dollar Motel (not Dollar60 Motel).

The next indexing rules are guides to filing records to and from agencies of (1) the United States government; (2) states, cities, and counties in the United States; and (3) foreign governments. Indexing the names of government units is easier if you remember that there is a difference between the function of a government agency and the designation of the office under which that function is carried out. Examples of functions are agriculture, commerce, defense, education, health, natural resources, planning, police, recreation, transportation, and welfare. Examples of the designation of an office are agency, board, bureau, commission, department, division, ministry, office, and service.

## Rule 11: Government Names

Government names are indexed first by the name of the country, state, county, or city under which the agency operates; then by the function; and then by the designation of the office. For example, in the name *Iowa Department of Education, Iowa* is the first unit because *Iowa* is the name of the state under which the Department of Education functions. *Education* is the second unit because education is a function or activity. *Department* is the third unit because it is the designation of the office under which the function is carried out. The fourth unit is *of*.

*Hint:* If you have trouble recognizing or indexing government names, it might help to look in the Blue Pages, if available, of a telephone directory. The Blue Pages contain listings for local, county, state, and United States government names.

United States government names are indexed first under United States Government. In each of the following examples of United States government names, Unit 1 is *United*, Unit 2 is *States*, and Unit 3 is *Government*.

| **Name** | **Name as Indexed** |
| --- | --- |
| U.S. Department of Agriculture Forest Service | United States Government Agriculture Department of Forest Service |
| U.S. Treasury Department Customs Service | United States Government Treasury Department Customs Service |
| U.S. Treasury Department Internal Revenue Service | United States Government Treasury Department Internal Revenue Service |

Following are examples of state and local government names.

| **Name** | **Name as Indexed** |
| --- | --- |
| Board of Education City of Freeport, Maine | Freeport City of Education Board of Freeport Maine |
| Bureau of Weights and Measures State of Maine Augusta, Maine | Maine State of Weights and Measures Bureau of Augusta Maine |
| Oregon Department of Education Salem, Oregon | Oregon Education Department of Salem Oregon |

| Name | Name as Indexed |
|---|---|
| Water Department | Stafford County |
| Stafford County | Water Department |
| Stafford, Virginia | Stafford Virginia |

Following are examples of foreign government names.

| Name | Name as Indexed |
|---|---|
| Ministry of Agriculture | Tunisia Republic of |
| Republic of Tunisia | Agriculture Ministry of |
| | |
| Department of Natural Resources | Venezuela Republic of |
| Republic of Venezuela | Natural Resources |
| | Department of |

## Rule 12: Identical Names

When names are otherwise identical, they may be filed by address. The elements of the address are considered in the following order: city, state (spelled in full), street name, and house or building number.

| Name | Unit 1 | Unit 2 | Unit 3 | Unit 4 | Unit 5 | Unit 6 |
|---|---|---|---|---|---|---|
| Videoworld<br>142 Broadway<br>Huntsville, AL 35813-0230 | Videoworld | Huntsville | Alabama | Broadway | 142 | |
| Videoworld<br>3600 South Main<br>Springfield, IL 62703-1408 | Videoworld | Springfield | Illinois | South | Main | 3600 |
| Videoworld<br>275 Hunter Circle<br>Springfield, MO 65801-1793 | Videoworld | Springfield | Missouri | Hunter | Circle | 275 |
| Videoworld<br>427 Lake Street<br>Toledo, OH 43601-1264 | Videoworld | Toledo | Ohio | Lake | Street | 427 |
| Videoworld<br>110 Norris Avenue<br>Toledo, OH 43601-0443 | Videoworld | Toledo | Ohio | Norris | Avenue | 110 |
| Videoworld<br>1400 Norris Avenue<br>Toledo, OH 43601-0445 | Videoworld | Toledo | Ohio | Norris | Avenue | 1400 |

*Note:* When addresses are otherwise identical, the house or building number is considered in numeric order. Therefore, for the last two names in the above examples, 110 is filed before 1400.

# MATERIALS FOR FILING PROJECTS

- **Filing Cards**
- **Correspondence Items 1–12**
- **Cross-Reference Sheets**
- **Correspondence Items 13–24**
- **Extra Cross-Reference Sheets**
- **Answer Sheets, Assignments 1–11**

| No. | Code | Description | Supplier | Cost | Price | Qty | Total |
|---|---|---|---|---|---|---|---|
| 129 | D2-0157 | VISIBLE FRAME 12 × 8 | Torrence File Products | 14.11 | 25.20 | 6 | 84.66 |
| 130 | B1-0216 | 2 DRAWER FILE, LETTER | Steel Furniture Company | 98.02 | 169.00 | 12 | 1,176.24 |
| 131 | E2-0467 | CATALOG CASE | Fancini Products | 43.16 | 83.00 | 2 | 86.32 |
| 132 | A2-0188 | EXECUTIVE DESK | Steel Furniture Company | 463.86 | 859.00 | 4 | 1,855.44 |
| 133 | D2-0453 | VISIBLE FILE 10 TRAY | Torrence File Products | 412.72 | 737.00 | 0 | 0.00 |
| 134 | C1-0153 | TELEPHONE LIST FINDER | Superior Office Products | 14.30 | 22.70 | 18 | 257.40 |
| 135 | D1-0124 | BUSINESS CARD FILE | Data Case Enterprises | 10.05 | 17.95 | 68 | 683.40 |
| 136 | C2-0398 | SHALLOW COIN TRAY | Romero Manufacturing Co. | 3.50 | 5.55 | 40 | 140.00 |

| No. | Code | Description | Supplier | Cost | Price | Qty | Total |
|---|---|---|---|---|---|---|---|
| 137 | E1-0245 | ULTIMA VINYL ATTACHE | United Luggage | 58.24 | 112.00 | 16 | 931.84 D2-0157 |
| 138 | B3-0398 | MOBILE SECURITY CABINET | DCR Business Equipment | 212.86 | 367.00 | 0 | 0.00 |
| 139 | A1-0135 | MICROCOMPUTER TABLE | Data Case Enterprises | 150.66 | 279.00 | 12 | 1,807.92 |
| 140 | D1-0333 | DATA FILE 3 × 5 | Data Case Enterprises | 12.25 | 21.88 | 16 | 196.00 |
| 141 | C1-0385 | PHONE LOCK | DCR Business Equipment | 4.00 | 6.35 | 15 | 60.00 |
| 142 | E3-0258 | DISK PACK CARRYING CASE | Data Case Enterprises | 74.10 | 142.50 | 5 | 370.50 |
| 143 | A3-0344 | PNEUMATIC TASK CHAIR | Steel Furniture Company | 68.58 | 127.00 | 6 | 411.48 |
| 144 | D1-0284 | ROTARY CARD FILE 4 × 6 | Visual Display Inc. | 53.06 | 94.75 | 21 | 1,114.26 |

| No. | Code | Description | Company | | | |
|---|---|---|---|---|---|---|
| 161 | B1-0196 | 3 DRAWER FILE, LETTER | Steel Furniture Company | 115.42 | 199.00 | 7 | 807.94 |
| 162 | B3-0236 | MOBILE PEDESTAL AND FILE | DCR Business Equipment | 172.84 | 298.00 | 4 | 691.36 |
| 163 | D1-0168 | DESKTOP VUE FILE | Data Case Enterprises | 9.07 | 16.20 | 13 | 117.91 |
| 164 | E1-0230 | PERFECTO LEATHER ATTACHE | United Luggage | 91.00 | 175.00 | 26 | 2,366.00 |
| 165 | B2-0174 | 4 DRAWER LATERAL FILE | Steel Furniture Company | 405.86 | 699.75 | 27 | 10,958.22 |
| 166 | A1-0157 | MICROCOMPUTER STAND | Data Case Enterprises | 48.06 | 89.00 | 6 | 288.36 |
| 167 | E2-0258 | SLIM UNDERARM PORTFOLIO | Fancini Products | 29.48 | 56.70 | 15 | 442.20 |
| 168 | B2-0184 | 3 DRAWER LATERAL FILE | Steel Furniture Company | 312.01 | 537.95 | 12 | 3,744.12 |
| 169 | A2-0315 | ADMINISTRATIVE DESK | DCR Business Equipment | 188.46 | 349.00 | 2 | 376.92 |
| 170 | D2-0389 | VISIBLE RECORD BOOK | Torrence File Products | 16.66 | 29.75 | 41 | 683.06 |
| 171 | C1-0317 | MINI PHONE SHOULDER REST | DCR Business Equipment | 3.40 | 5.39 | 26 | 88.40 |
| 172 | C1-0277 | TELEPHONE HEADSET | Superior Office Products | 18.87 | 29.95 | 15 | 283.05 |
| 173 | B3-0189 | PRINTOUT MOBILE FILE | DCR Business Equipment | 126.37 | 217.88 | 5 | 631.85 |
| 174 | A3-0279 | WORKSTATION CHAIR | Steel Furniture Company | 57.78 | 107.00 | 20 | 1,155.60 |
| 175 | E3-0237 | MAG TAPE CARRYING CASE | Data Case Enterprises | 42.12 | 81.00 | 0 | 0.00 |
| 176 | E2-0348 | ZIPAROUND PORTFOLIO | Fancini Products | 54.44 | 104.70 | 8 | 435.52 |

**153** — B2-0194 2 DRAWER LATERAL FILE
Steel Furniture Company
242.41 417.95 4 969.64

**154** — A2-0299 LATERAL FILE
Steel Furniture Company
292.68 542.00 18 5,268.24

**155** — D1-0425 CLOSED ROTARY FILE
Romero Manufacturing Co.
20.69 36.95 12 248.28

**156** — A1-0327 PRINTER STAND
Data Case Enterprises
90.45 167.50 7 633.15

**157** — A1-0233 BI-LEVEL COMPUTER STAND
Steel Furniture Company
83.70 155.00 7 585.90

**158** — D2-0463 VISIBLE FILE 17 TRAY
Torrence File Products
665.84 1,189.00 0 0.00

**159** — B3-0266 DESKTOP FILE
DCR Business Equipment
28.71 49.50 18 516.78

**160** — C1-0422 MESSAGE HOLDER
DCR Business Equipment
2.32 3.69 196 454.72

**145** — A3-0256 TASK CHAIR
Superior Office Products
72.63 134.50 140 10,168.20

**146** — E1-0265 ULTIMA LEATHER ATTACHE
United Luggage
111.77 214.95 17 1,900.09

**147** — C2-0273 COLOR-KEYED COIN TUBE SET
Romero Manufacturing Co.
17.96 28.50 9 161.64

**148** — D2-0147 VISIBLE FRAME 12 × 6
Torrence File Products
13.27 23.70 8 106.16

**149** — B1-0156 5 DRAWER FILE, LETTER
Steel Furniture Company
190.82 329.00 18 3,434.76

**150** — D1-0137 DESKTOP TRAY FILE
Data Case Enterprises
10.36 18.50 55 569.80

**151** — C1-0246 TELEPHONE SHOULDER REST
Superior Office Products
6.23 9.89 34 211.82

**152** — E3-0198 CARTRIDGE CARRYING CASE
Data Case Enterprises
41.55 79.90 6 249.30

| Code | Description | Supplier | Cost | Price | Qty | Total | |
|---|---|---|---|---|---|---|---|
| C1-0114 | TELEPHONE INDEX | Superior Office Products | 13.39 | 21.25 | 27 | 361.53 | |
| B1-0176 | 4 DRAWER FILE, LETTER | Steel Furniture Company | 137.46 | 237.00 | 14 | 1,924.44 | |
| A2-0267 | CREDENZA | Steel Furniture Company | 399.33 | 739.50 | 2 | 798.66 | |
| C2-0246 | CASH DRAWER | Romero Manufacturing Co. | 99.86 | 158.50 | 3 | 299.58 | |
| A1-0359 | PAPER FEED TRAY | Steel Furniture Company | 18.63 | 34.50 | 8 | 149.04 | |
| A2-0334 | COMPACT DESK | DCR Business Equipment | 143.91 | 266.50 | 6 | 863.46 | |
| E1-0168 | RENWAY VINYL ATTACHE | United Luggage | 34.06 | 65.50 | 30 | 1,021.80 | |
| C2-0349 | COUNTER CHANGE TRAY | Romero Manufacturing Co. | 22.52 | 35.75 | 0 | 0.00 | |
| 177 | D1-0323 | DATA FILE 2.25 × 4 | Data Case Enterprises | 10.63 | 18.98 | 6 | 63.78 |
| 178 | D1-0225 | COVERED SWIVEL FILE | Data Case Enterprises | 20.13 | 35.95 | 19 | 382.47 |
| 179 | C2-0235 | CASH BOX | Romero Manufacturing Co. | 24.54 | 38.95 | 12 | 294.48 |
| 180 | C1-0368 | PHONE CUSHION | DCR Business Equipment | 1.00 | 1.59 | 77 | 77.00 |
| 181 | C2-0388 | DEEP COIN TRAY | Romero Manufacturing Company | 5.01 | 7.95 | 12 | 60.12 |
| 182 | B3-0153 | DESK SIDE MOBILE FILE | DCR Business Equipment | 74.44 | 128.35 | 8 | 595.52 |
| 183 | D1-0274 | ROTARY CARD FILE 3 x 5 | Visual Display Inc. | 18.45 | 32.95 | 14 | 258.30 |
| 184 | A3-0421 | ERGONOMIC CHAIR | Steel Furniture Company | 194.27 | 359.75 | 0 | 0.00 |

185  186  187  188  189  190  191  192

# Regal Leathers
218 Commonwealth Avenue
Boston, MA 02116-0782

July 28, 20--

Ahmal Jackson
Scorcher Athletics, Inc.
374 Quincy Market Road
Boston, MA 02109-1476

Dear Mr. Jackson:

I would like to arrange a time, as soon as possible, to display for you some samples of our new treated leather. We can then discuss marketing efforts and information needed for your advertising.

After a year of research and development, Regal Leathers has developed a new leather treatment at the Milford plant that was federally approved on July 25, 20--. This leather treatment is a combination of environmentally safe chemicals that has improved the quality of the leather. Treatment with this new product gives the leather increased softness, flexibility, and durability.

I am suggesting that this new leather treatment be applied to your new running shoe design and that it be introduced as the "Envirun" shoe.

Sincerely,

Laressa Washington
Sales Representative

tw

---

# Regal Leathers
218 Commonwealth Avenue
Boston, MA 02116-0782

July 28, 20--

Roxanne Knight
Scorcher Athletics, Inc.
374 Quincy Market Road
Boston, MA 02109-1476

Dear Ms. Knight:

Payment is due on Monday, August 14, 20-- for Regular Stock Leather No. 92384 for the month of July.

| Description | Quantity | Cost per Cut Sheet | Total |
| --- | --- | --- | --- |
| Reg. Stock Leather No. 92384 | 200 | $90.00 | $18,000.00 |
| Total Payment Due | | | $18,000.00 |

Sincerely,

Amy Hart
Accounts Receivable

tw

# SPECIALTY OFFICE SUPPLY COMPANY

6940 NORTH MAIN STREET
MEMPHIS, TN 38112-1704

August 1, 20 --

Roxanne Knight
Scorcher Athletics, Inc.
374 Quincy Market Road
Boston, MA 02109-1476

Dear Ms. Knight:

Are you tired of the same old office decor? Then add some variety with our novelty line of office wallpaper, cups, pens, pencils, posters, and calendars. Call now for more information: 1-800-555-5959.

Cordially,

David Wang

David Wang
Sales Representative

gl

---

*Sports & Weights Unlimited*
45 University Drive • Cambridge MA 02138-1318

August 2, 20 --

Roxanne Knight
Scorcher Athletics, Inc.
374 Quincy Market Road
Boston, MA 02109-1476

Dear Ms. Knight:

This letter is just a reminder for you that Sports & Weights Unlimited will be closed on Labor Day and will resume business as usual the next day.

Sincerely,

James Black

James Black
Personnel Director

rp

## Scorcher
Athletics, Inc.
374 Quincy Market Road
Boston, MA 02109-1476

August 3, 20 --

FAX TO: 617-555-3890

Laressa Washington
Sales Representative
Regal Leathers
218 Commonwealth Avenue
Boston, MA 02116-0782

Dear Ms. Washington:

Subject: MARKETING NEW LEATHER TREATMENT

On Monday, August 7, 20 -- at 9:00 a.m., I will reserve an hour for your presentation on your new leather treatment. If this new process gives the leather the characteristics you report, I might decide to use it for our new running shoe. We can discuss the details in person on Monday morning.

Sincerely,

*Ahmal Jackson*

Ahmal Jackson
President

aj

---

## Scorcher
Athletics, Inc.
374 Quincy Market Road
Boston, MA 02109-1476

August 7, 20 --

Frances Choi
Sports & Weights Unlimited
45 University Drive
Cambridge, MA 02138-1318

Dear Frances:

Subject: PAYMENT DUE US

We have not yet received payment for Scorcher products that were shipped to you during the month of June. You should have received our invoice for these products by July 7. Because you have been such a good customer, we will honor our usual 30-day discount policy if we receive your payment by August 14.

Sincerely,

*Roxanne Knight*

Roxanne Knight
Vice President for Production

rk

*Scorcher*
Athletics, Inc.
374 Quincy Market Road
Boston, MA 02109-1476

August 8, 20 – –

Gary Osborn
Production Director
Regal Leathers
218 Commonwealth Avenue
Boston, MA 02116-0782

Dear Gary:

Subject: LEATHER SPECIFICATIONS

Our president, Ahmal Jackson, has given his approval for the use of your new leather treatment for our new running shoe and for naming this shoe the Envirun shoe. Please propose an amendment to our service contract to include the new leather treatment specifications with costs, stock numbers, terms, and procedures.

Sincerely,

*Roxanne Knight*

Roxanne Knight
Vice President for Production

rk

---

*Scorcher*
Athletics, Inc.
374 Quincy Market Road
Boston, MA 02109-1476

August 8, 20 – –

Carmon Ladd
Chief of Shipping
Reggie's Trucking Company
9361 Newbury Street
Boston, MA 02115-1388

Dear Ms. Ladd:

Subject: TRANSPORTING NEW PRODUCTS

Scorcher will be using Regal Leathers' new leather treatment made at their Milford, Massachusetts, plant for our new running shoe design called the Envirun shoe. This requires adding another pickup route. Can your company add this new route beginning August 21, 20 – –, for delivery to Sportswear Sewing Center in Worcester, Massachusetts, with the same pickup times as those previously used for the Newton plant?

Sincerely,

*Roxanne Knight*

Roxanne Knight
Vice President for Production

rk

**Scorcher**
Athletics, Inc.
374 Quincy Market Road
Boston, MA 02109-1476

August 9, 20 --

Taylor Johnson, President
Sportswear Sewing Center
2800 Industrial Road
Worcester, MA 02178-1246

Dear Mr. Johnson:

Subject: DESIGN SPECIFICATIONS

I am pleased to inform you about the new leather treatment that has been chosen for our new running shoe design to be called the Envirun shoe. This new leather treatment uses federally approved and environmentally safe chemical compounds that increase the leather's softness, flexibility, and durability. Scorcher's logo will use the colors of kelly green and medium brown to represent the environmentally conscious product.

Is it possible to have our logo embroidered, rather than glued, onto the shoe? If this can be done, we would like you to do so.

Sincerely,

Ahmal Jackson

Ahmal Jackson
President

aj

**Scorcher**
Athletics, Inc.
374 Quincy Market Road
Boston, MA 02109-1476

August 11, 20 --

Bruce Richards
Construction Supervisor
Sportswear Sewing Center
2800 Industrial Road
Worcester, MA 02178-1246

Dear Bruce:

Subject: MATERIALS SPECIFICATIONS

We have chosen a new leather treatment for our new running shoe design to be called the Envirun shoe. This new leather treatment uses federally approved and environmentally safe chemical compounds that increase the leather's softness, flexibility, and durability.

Because of changes in the characteristics of the leather, we have determined that Sportswear Sewing Center should change to thread number 3205 for the Envirun shoe instead of the usual thread number 5698.

Cordially,

Roxanne Knight

Roxanne Knight
Vice President for Production

rk

*Scorcher*
Athletics, Inc.
374 Quincy Market Road
Boston, MA 02109-1476

August 11, 20 --

Bill Shore
Head Dispatcher
Reggie's Trucking Company
9361 Newbury Street
Boston, MA 02115-1388

Dear Bill:

Subject: POSSIBLE TRANSPORTATION DELAYS

This notice is to alert you and the other dispatchers that the new route you will be using to pick up materials at Regal Leathers in Milford, Massachusetts, has a lot of highway construction in progress. The construction is expected to last for at least six months.

Please caution your drivers to allow extra time when traveling this route.

Sincerely,

*Roxanne Knight*

Roxanne Knight
Vice President for Production

rk

---

*Reggie's* TRUCKING
COMPANY
9361 NEWBURY STREET • BOSTON, MA 02115-1388

August 11, 20 --

Roxanne Knight
Scorcher Athletics, Inc.
374 Quincy Market Road
Boston, MA 02109-1476

Dear Ms. Knight:

Yes, Reggie's Trucking Company can add the new pickup route with the same pickup times beginning August 21, 20 --. Thank you for continuing to choose Reggie's Trucking Company for your trucking service.

Cordially,

*Carmon Ladd*

Carmon Ladd
Chief of Shipping

fl

# CROSS-REFERENCE SHEET

Name _____    File No. _____

Date _____    Regarding _____

## SEE:

Name _____    File No. _____

---

# CROSS-REFERENCE SHEET

Name _____    File No. _____

Date _____    Regarding _____

## SEE:

Name _____    File No. _____

*Sportswear Sewing Center*
*2800 Industrial Road*
*Worcester, MA 02178-1246*

August 11, 20--

Ahmal Jackson
Scorcher Athletics, Inc.
374 Quincy Market Road
Boston, MA 02109-1476

Dear Mr. Jackson:

I am delighted to hear about the Envirun shoe and to be doing business with an environmentally conscious organization such as yours.

In response to your request, we can embroider the Scorcher logo onto this shoe. I have told the construction supervisor to include this adjustment in the design specifications.

Sincerely,

Taylor Johnson
President

el

---

**Tough-Tear Nylon Company**
5042 Beacon Street
Cambridge, MA 02138-0814

August 11, 20--

Ahmal Jackson
Scorcher Athletics, Inc.
374 Quincy Market Road
Boston, MA 02109-1476

Dear Mr. Jackson:

Thank you for marketing our latest sportswear design to match your new Envirun shoe line. The enclosed sketches and samples will show you that the clothing style is as equally sleek-looking, comfortable, and durable as the shoe. I believe this design ranks among the best in sportswear fashion.

Please phone me at 555-6237 to give me your reaction to these designs. We will then prepare advertising copy for your approval.

Sincerely,

Tanya Jones
Sportswear Designer

tj

Enclosures

FAX TO:617-555-8532   FROM: 617-555-9344   10:14a.m.

**Tough-Tear**
**Nylon**
**Company**   5042 Beacon Street
Cambridge, MA 02138-0814

August 15, 20 --

Ahmal Jackson
Scorcher Athletics, Inc.
374 Quincy Market Road
Boston, MA 02109-1476

Dear Mr. Jackson:

I would like to arrange a time as soon as possible to discuss the coordinated marketing of our new line of sportswear that will match your new Envirun shoe. Please notify me of your earliest available date so we can set up a meeting. Thank you.

Sincerely,

David Kim

David Kim
Sales Representative

dk

---

*Scorcher*
Athletics, Inc.
374 Quincy Market Road
Boston, MA 02109-1476

August 15, 20 --

FAX TO: 617-555-9344

David Kim
Sales Representative
Tough-Tear Nylon Company
5042 Beacon Street
Cambridge, MA 02138-0814

Dear Mr. Kim:

Subject: COMBINED MARKETING EFFORT

I will be available to meet with you on Thursday, August 17, at 2:00 p.m., to see your new line of sportswear. If it coordinates well with our new Envirun shoes, we can plan a cooperative marketing effort.

Sincerely,

Ahmal Jackson

Ahmal Jackson
President

aj

## Letter 1 (page 17)

*Sportswear Sewing Center*
*2800 Industrial Road*
*Worcester, MA 02178-1246*

August 14, 20 --

Roxanne Knight
Scorcher Athletics, Inc.
374 Quincy Market Road
Boston, MA 02109-1476

Dear Ms. Knight:

Payment is due on Friday, August 25, 20 -- for sports shoes numbers 14789, 83498, 68789, and 47929 and for sportswear design numbers S75892, S78589, and S77809 for the time period of August 1 to 15, 20 --. Refer to invoices 16-486 and 16-493 for the specific quantities and amounts.

Sincerely,

Maria Sanchez

Maria Sanchez
Accounts Receivable

tw

## Letter 2 (page 18)

*Sportswear Sewing Center*
*2800 Industrial Road*
*Worcester, MA 02178-1246*

August 15, 20 --

Roxanne Knight
Scorcher Athletics, Inc.
374 Quincy Market Road
Boston, MA 02109-1476

Dear Ms. Knight:

Thank you for the information about the new leather to be used in your Envirun shoes. As you requested, we will change our specifications to indicate the use of thread number 3205 rather than thread number 5698.

Sincerely,

Bruce Richards

Bruce Richards
Construction Supervisor

rt

## Reggie's TRUCKING COMPANY

9361 NEWBURY STREET • BOSTON, MA 02115-1388

August 16, 20 --

Roxanne Knight
Scorcher Athletics, Inc.
374 Quincy Market Road
Boston, MA 02109-1476

Dear Ms. Knight:

I received from Carmon Ladd and Bill Shore your information about the new route that will be needed to pick up materials from the Regal Leathers plant in Milford.

All of our drivers have received the new schedules and directions to the plant, as well as information on precautionary measures they may need to take because of the highway construction.

Cordially,

Todd Franks

Todd Franks
Dispatching Coordinator

tf

---

## Scorcher

Athletics, Inc.
374 Quincy Market Road
Boston, MA 02109-1476

August 18, 20 --

Rhonda Goldberg
Advertising Director
Sports & Weights Unlimited
45 University Drive
Cambridge, MA 02138-1318

Dear Rhonda:

Subject: MARKETING NEW SHOE LINE

Scorcher's new line of running shoes will be ready for your store on October 1. We appreciate your eagerness to help us test market this new product. The line will be called Envirun and will feature a leather treatment that uses environmentally safe chemical compounds. This innovative treatment was recently developed by Regal Leathers.

In late September, we will send you display posters and ad copy for print advertisements featuring the Envirun shoes. We look forward to receiving sales reports and suggestions for future marketing efforts.

Sincerely,

Roxanne Knight

Roxanne Knight
Vice President for Production

rk

*Sports & Weights Unlimited*
45 University Drive • Cambridge MA 02138-1318

August 23, 20 --

Roxanne Knight
Scorcher Athletics, Inc.
374 Quincy Market Road
Boston, MA 02109-1476

Dear Ms. Knight:

Sports & Weights Unlimited will begin an aggressive marketing campaign for your new Envirun line of running shoes starting October 1. If you have sample models available before that time, an advance display could be set up to build customer interest.

Could either you or Regal Leathers send us more information about the environmental aspects of the leather treatment compound? We would like to develop advertising that promotes this feature of the Envirun shoes.

Sincerely,

Rhonda Goldberg

Rhonda Goldberg
Advertising Director

aw

---

**Tough-Tear Nylon Company**
5042 Beacon Street
Cambridge, MA 02138-0814

August 24, 20 --

Roxanne Knight
Scorcher Athletics, Inc.
374 Quincy Market Road
Boston, MA 02109-1476

Dear Ms. Knight:

The purpose of this letter is to inform you that your previous contact here, Andy Wassman, recently left the company to pursue further education.

I look forward to continuing to work with you.

Cordially,

Rashad Ahmed

Rashad Ahmed
Accounts Receivable

dl

**Tough-Tear**
**Nylon**
**Company** 5042 Beacon Street
Cambridge, MA 02138-0814

August 31, 20 --

Roxanne Knight
Scorcher Athletics, Inc.
374 Quincy Market Road
Boston, MA 02109-1476

Dear Ms. Knight:

Payment for the materials you received from Tough-Tear during the month of August will be due by September 15. Included are invoice numbers 1692, 1808, 2148, 2212, and 2558.

We appreciate your continued business and prompt payment.

Cordially,

Rashad Ahmed

Rashad Ahmed
Accounts Receivable

dl

---

**Sure-Credit, Inc.**
P.O. BOX 1535
HACKENSACK, NJ 07606-1535

August 28, 20 --

Roxanne Knight
Scorcher Athletics, Inc.
374 Quincy Market Road
Boston, MA 02109-1476

Dear Ms. Knight:

Because of your excellent credit record, Sure-Credit is pleased to inform you that you have pre-approval to receive a $5,000 credit limit with your new credit card from us. This card can be used at many retail stores in Boston and throughout Massachusetts.

The yearly fee for your Sure-Credit is $25, and the annual interest rate for charges not paid within 30 days is 22%. Just complete and return the enclosed form to receive your card.

Sincerely,

Joe Stevens

Joe Stevens
Sales Representative

vm

Enc.

# CROSS-REFERENCE SHEET

Name

File No. _____

Regarding

Date _____

## SEE:

Name

File No. _____

---

# CROSS-REFERENCE SHEET

Name

File No. _____

Regarding

Date _____

## SEE:

Name

File No. _____

Answer Sheet    Name _Sherese Prentes_

Date _5-18-07_

Assignment 3A
Numeric Filing

0000–0999  _25, 3, 27, 28, 2, 21_

1000–1999  _26, 20, 29, 13, 12_

2000–2999  _19, 10, 11, 9, 17, 31, 30, 18, 8, 22, 6_

3000–3999  _14, 16, 32, 5, 1_

4000–4999  _7, 23, 15, 4, 24_

---

Answer Sheet    Name _Sherese Prentes_

Date _____

Assignment 1
Alphabetic Filing
Individual Names

A–D  _12, 19, 10_

E–I  _24, 32, 22, 3, 25, 4, 25, 13, 12, 5, 4, 13, 31_

J–O  _6, 11, 14, 26, 18, 30, 27_

P–T  _29, 15, 23, 17, 28_

U–Z  _8, 16, 9, 21, 7, 20_

---

Answer Sheet    Name _Sherese Prentes_

Date _5-18-07_

Assignment 3B
Numeric Filing

0000–0999  _61, 38, 50, 35, 39, 55, 56_

1000–1999  _56, 45, 41, 37, 33, 42, 47, 49_

2000–2999  _54, 36_

3000–3999  _57, 52, 40, 51, 63, 46, 48_

4000–4999  _58, 62, 60, 53, 43, 64, 44, 34_

---

Answer Sheet    Name _Sherese Prentes_

Date _5-18-07_

Assignment 2
Alphabetic Filing
Individual Names

A–D  _60, 43, 41, 39, 57, 61, 48, 34, 61, 59_

E–I  _60, 44, 35, 49, 55, 53_

J–O  _44, 42, 51, 54, 46, 29_

P–T  _44, 59, 37_

U–Z  _47, 45, 56, 33, 63, 38_

Answer Sheet    Name _____

Date _____

Assignment 6B
Geographic Filing

NC REGION _____

NE REGION _____

NW REGION _____

SC REGION _____

SE REGION _____

Answer Sheet    Name *Theresa Puentes*

Date *June 8, 2007*

Assignment 5
Alphabetic Filing
Business Names

A–D _____

E–I _____

J–O _____

P–T _____

U–Z _____

---

Answer Sheet    Name _____

Date _____

Assignment 6A
Geographic Filing

NC REGION _75_

NE REGION _____

NW REGION _____

SC REGION _____

SE REGION _____

Answer Sheet    Name *Theresa Puentes*

Date *June 8, 2007*

Assignment 4
Alphabetic Filing
Business Names

A–D 73,79,86,83

E–I 65,80,95

J–O 74,67,69,81,90

P–T 91,91,68,78,70,87,82,76,93,85,88,84, 78,82,91

U–Z 77,92,95,96,84

Assignment 8
Project Quiz

Alphabetizing Names of Individuals (6 points each, total 30 points)

1. _____

2. _____

3. _____

4. _____

5. _____

Numeric Filing (5 points each, total 10 points)

6. _____

7. _____

Alphabetizing Business and Organization Names (6 points each, total 30 points)

8. _____

9. _____

10. _____

11. _____

12. _____

Over for questions 13 through 19

---

Answer Sheet    Name _____

Date _____

Assignment 7B
Subject Filing

A—FURNITURE _____

B—FILE CABINETS _____

C—ACCESSORIES _____

D—VISIBILE FILES _____

E—CARRIERS _____

---

Answer Sheet    Name _____

Date _____

Assignment 7A
Subject Filing

A—FURNITURE _____

B—FILE CABINETS _____

C—ACCESSORIES _____

D—VISIBILE FILES _____

E—CARRIERS _____

Assignment 8    Project Quiz (continued)

Geographic Filing (4 points each, total 20 points)

13. _____

14. _____

15. _____

16. _____

17. _____

Subject Filing (5 points each, total 10 points)

18. _____

19. _____

Name _____

Date _____

| Item No. | Discard? | | Alphabetic Caption | Action |
|---|---|---|---|---|
| | **Yes** | **No** | | |
| 1 | | X | Regal Leathers | Route to Vice President; File |
| 2 | | | | |
| 3 | | | | |
| 4 | | | | |
| 5 | | | | |
| 6 | | | | |
| 7 | | | | |
| 8 | | | | |
| 9 | | | | |
| 10 | | | | |
| 11 | | | | |
| 12 | | | | |

Answer Sheet     Name _____

                 Date _____

Assignment 9B: Receipt and Creation of Correspondence

| Item No. | Discard? | | Alphabetic Caption | Action |
|---|---|---|---|---|
| | Yes | No | | |
| 13 | | | | |
| 14 | | | | |
| 15 | | | | |
| 16 | | | | |
| 17 | | | | |
| 18 | | | | |
| 19 | | | | |
| 20 | | | | |
| 21 | | | | |
| 22 | | | | |
| 23 | | | | |
| 24 | | | | |

Answer Sheet    Name _____

Date _____

Assignment 10
Alphabetic Correspondence Filing

Regal Leathers                    _21x_

Reggie's Trucking Company    _____

Sports & Weights Unlimited    _____

Sportswear Sewing Center     _____

Tough-Tear Nylon Company    _____


Answer Sheet    Name _____

Date _____

Assignment 11
Subject Correspondence Filing

Accounts Payable              _24_

Accounts Receivable          _____

Marketing and Advertising    _____

Specifications               _____

Transportation               _____

# DATABASE PROJECTS

## Introduction

A *database* is a body of organized data, usually managed in a computer system, that can be modified, reorganized, and accessed in various ways to carry out administrative tasks and to solve business problems. Within a database, information is stored in *tables*. An example of a table is a collection of information about all the customers of a business. Each item in a table is called a *record*. For example, in a customer table, there is one record for each customer. Records contain information that is divided into categories called *fields*. An example of information in a field of a customer's record is 4738, the customer's account number.

As with paper files, if you want to look up information in a database, first you must know something unique about the record you are looking for. For example, if you are searching for a customer's record, you must know the customer's name or account number—information that is unique to the customer. Fields that are called *key fields* must contain unique information. Every record must have one or more key fields so that a specific record can be found when it is needed.

The first two database projects allow you to work with computer files that have been entered onto the data disk accompanying this practice set. The third project challenges you to design and establish a new database for a small firm. The three projects are:

Project Three: Jacobsen's Department Store
A retail customer database with 200 customers

Project Four: New Age Office Supply
A retail inventory database with 200 products

Project Five: NighTech Restaurant
An employee database with 24 employees

At the end of each database project is a project quiz. Each quiz is based on what you have learned in the project and includes questions that you answer by looking at database information on your computer screen. The quizzes were prepared under the assumption that all assignments prior to the quiz were completed correctly or were corrected. To ensure the accuracy of your database prior to taking the quiz, check your data against the printouts provided by your instructor.

# Instructions for Using the Disk

The assignments in Project Three and Project Four assume that you make changes to the database files.

The accompanying CD contains the files for the database projects and are recorded in Microsoft Access 97 format.

To use the practice files:

1. If your computer does *not* have Microsoft Access installed, install a copy of Microsoft Access 97 or Microsoft Access 2000 on your computer.
   **Note:** You can use a different database program provided it can import and convert Microsoft Access 97 databases. However, the instructions here are geared for students using Microsoft Access 97 only.

2. Insert the CD into the CD-ROM drive of your computer.

3. Open the Windows Explorer and click on the **D:** drive (or the drive letter associated with your CD-ROM drive).

4. Select the files and copy them to an appropriate folder on your computer's hard drive.

5. Select each file, right click, and choose "Properties" from the shortcut menu. Under the "Attributes" section at the bottom of the "General" tab's panel, make sure that the "Read-Only" box is *not* checked. If it is, click on the check mark to remove it.

6. Click OK.

7. Once the files have been set for writing, open the files that have been copied to the hard drive. Open the file by selecting the folder you copied the practice files to and double click on the appropriate file: Project3.mdb for Assignments 13-21 and Project4.mdb for Assignments 22-32.
   **Note:** Project Five (Assignments 33-40) does not have a practice file. You must create this database from scratch.

8. If you are using Access 2000, you will be asked whether or not your want to convert the database.
   **Choose YES.** You will then be asked to choose a new name for the database.
   **Type** Project 3_2000.mdb for Project Three.
   **Type** Project 4_2000.mdb for Project Four.

9. Proceed with the assignments that follow.

   *Note:* If you are using Microsoft Access 2000, some of the screens will look different from the way they look in this workbook. However, the instructions should provide enough guidance to allow you to complete the projects.

# PROJECT THREE  Jacobsen's Department Store

## Assignment 13: Explore the Customer Database Table

Follow your instructor's directions and install the database on your lab computer. Open the database and click on the tab that says TABLES. Click on the PROJECT3 table, and then click Open. You can now view all the information collected for the Jacobsen's Department Store customer database table.

1. What are the names of the fields? (The first field is given as an example.)

| Field Names | Field Names |
|---|---|
| *AccountNumber* | |
| | |
| | |
| | |
| | |

2. How many digits are in each account number?

2. _____

3. What is the name of the customer whose account number is 1301?

3. _____

4. Each customer's name is entered in the name field in address, or standard, order. It is entered again in the IndexedName field in indexed order. Indexed order means that a person's name has been transposed and has been written in capital letters, and the punctuation has been deleted. The purpose of the IndexedName field is to enable the user to sort names into the correct alphabetical order. Find account number 2075. What is the indexed name of this customer?

4. _____

5. What is the address of the customer whose account number is 1192?

5. _____

6. All of the customers live in Illinois (IL) or Missouri (MO). The customer whose account number is 3037 lives in which state?

6. _____

**7.** The last four digits of the zip code are called the zip code extension. What is the zip code extension of the customer whose account number is 1806?

7. _____

**8.** The first three digits of the Phone field make up the area code. What is the area code of the customer whose account number is 2297?

8. _____

**9.** Each customer has a credit limit. The credit limit is the balance that a customer's account may not exceed. The lowest credit limit in the customer table is $500, and the limits increase in $250 increments to a maximum credit limit of $2000. What is the credit limit of the customer whose account number is 3016?

9. _____

**10.** In the CreditRating field, each customer is given a rating of A, B, or C, depending on how promptly the customer pays his or her monthly bill. A rating of A means excellent, B means good, and C means fair. Does the customer with account number 2338 have an excellent credit rating?

10. _____

Name _____ Date_____ Score ____

## PROJECT THREE

# Jacobsen's Department Store

## Assignment 14: Make Changes to the Database Table

Open the Project Three database and click on the tab that says TABLES. Click on the PROJECT3 table and click Open. For each of the following, select the record with the AccountNumber shown and make the indicated change to the record. After you have made each change, document it by writing the name (or changed name) of the customer for whom the change was made. The first item is an example for an alteration that has already been made.

| Account Number | Change | Name |
|---|---|---|
| **0.** 2528 | Credit limit to $1000 | **0.** _Chang-Hong Wu_ |
| **1.** 0982 | Phone to 314-555-8894 | **1.** _____ |
| **2.** 2968 | Name to Samuel L. Fong and IndexedName to FONG SAMUEL L | **2.** _____ |
| **3.** 3032 | Credit rating to A | **3.** _____ |
| **4.** 2005 | Address to 1213 Deerfield Lane and zip code extension to 1609 | **4.** _____ |
| **5.** 1678 | Phone to 314-555-1434 | **5.** _____ |
| **6.** 1381 | Credit limit to $1500 | **6.** _____ |
| **7.** 1892 | Address to P.O. Box 1848 and zip code extension to 1848 | **7.** _____ |
| **8.** 0781 | Credit rating to B | **8.** _____ |
| **9.** 2268 | Name to Karen H. Krause-Daniels and IndexedName to KRAUSEDANIELS KAREN H | **9.** _____ |
| **10.** 2747 | Credit limit to $1750 and credit rating to B | **10.** _____ |

Name _____Date_____Score _____

# Jacobsen's Department Store

## Assignment 15: Delete Records from the Database Table

Open the Project Three database and click on the tab that says TABLES. Click on the PROJECT3 table and click Open. For each of the following, select and delete the record indicated by the AccountNumber. Document the fact by writing your initials in the Account Closed By column.

| Number of Account to Be Closed | Account Closed By |
|---|---|
| 1. 2867 | 1. _____ |
| 2. 0725 | 2. _____ |
| 3. 2089 | 3. _____ |
| 4. 1568 | 4. _____ |
| 5. 2311 | 5. _____ |

## PROJECT THREE

# Jacobsen's Department Store

## Assignment 16: Practice Indexing Names

One of your responsibilities is to establish records for new customers. Before you enter new records into a customer table, you will need to know how to write the customer names in indexed form so they can be keyed correctly in the IndexedName field. In this assignment, you will practice writing the names of individuals in indexed form. (If you are not familiar with the rules for indexing names of individuals, consult Chapter 5 in the textbook *Professional Records and Information Management,* Second Edition.)

Remember that indexed names of persons are transposed and keyed in all capital letters without punctuation. Examples of names and how they are written in indexed form follow.

| Name | Indexed Name |
|------|--------------|
| Roberta A. Wilson | WILSON ROBERTA A |
| Patrick M. O'Reilly | OREILLY PATRICK M |
| Kathy Von der Kellen | VONDERKELLEN KATHY |
| Huang R. Tsu-Wong | TSUWONG HUANG R |
| Dr. Hamed D. Rashad | RASHAD HAMED D DR |
| Elizabeth R. Doss, CPA | DOSS ELIZABETH R CPA |

Using the above examples as a guide, write the indexed form of each of the following names.

| Name | Indexed Name |
|------|--------------|
| 1. Martha F. Pinzon | 1. _____ |
| 2. Richard d'Angelo | 2. _____ |
| 3. Kirsten A. Van Camp | 3. _____ |
| 4. Warren E. Wise-Lockwood | 4. _____ |
| 5. Capt. Gail E. Coffey | 5. _____ |
| 6. Leslie G. Cinalli, Ph.D | 6. _____ |

| Name | Indexed Name |
|------|--------------|
| **7.** Ann-Marie Donally | **7.** _____ |
| **8.** Mohamed E. Pavlevi | **8.** _____ |
| **9.** Erin G. McAllister | **9.** _____ |
| **10.** Dorsey Wardlow, Jr. | **10.** _____ |

| PROJECT THREE | Jacobsen's Department Store |

## Assignment 17: Add Records to the Database

Ten new customers have opened charge accounts with Jacobsen's. Shown below are forms containing the account number for each new customer; the name, address, and phone number of each customer; and the credit limit and credit rating that have been assigned by the credit manager.

Open the Project Three database and click on the tab that says FORMS. Click on the form named AccountInfo and click Open. Add the ten new customers to the table. As you do so, determine the indexed name from the name that is given. Write the indexed name in the space provided on each form below. Remember that, to add a new record from the AccountInfo database form, click the New Record button in the record navigator at the bottom of the Form window. `Record: |◄ | ◄ | 1 | ► | ►| (►*) | of 30`

```
ACCOUNT #: 3038          NAME: Gregory T. Cooper
INDEXED NAME: _____
ADDRESS: 801 Ingalls Street          CITY: Granite City   STATE: IL
ZIP: 62040-1434   PHONE: 618-555-6238   CR LIMIT: $500.00  CR RATING: C


ACCOUNT #: 3039          NAME: Elizabeth D. Guynn
INDEXED NAME: _____
ADDRESS: 214 Fairfax Street          CITY: Ferguson      STATE: MO
ZIP: 63135-2413   PHONE: 314-555-7226   CR LIMIT: $1000.00 CR RATING: B


ACCOUNT #: 3040          NAME: Theresa D. Pryzby, MD
INDEXED NAME: _____
ADDRESS:  375 Clearview Drive        CITY: Spanish Lake   STATE: MO
ZIP: 63137-1255   PHONE: 314-555-8838   CR LIMIT: $1500.00 CR RATING: A


ACCOUNT #: 3041          NAME: Louis Heath-Camp
INDEXED NAME: _____
ADDRESS: PO Box 133                  CITY: St. Charles    STATE:  MO
ZIP: 63301-0133   PHONE: 314-555-8292   CR LIMIT: $750.00  CR RATING: B
```

ACCOUNT #: 3042            NAME: Kelly R. Von Dohlen

INDEXED NAME: _____

ADDRESS: 965 Cardinal Drive        CITY: Spanish Lake   STATE:  MO

ZIP: 63137-1348    PHONE: 314-555-7810   CR LIMIT: $1000.00 CR RATING: B


ACCOUNT #: 3043            NAME: Sean O'Hara

INDEXED NAME: _____

ADDRESS: 2803 Chelsea Court       CITY: Alton       STATE:  IL

ZIP: 62002-3291    PHONE: 618-555-9190   CR LIMIT:  $750.00 CR RATING:  C


ACCOUNT #: 3044            NAME: Marie H. Rojas

INDEXED NAME: _____

ADDRESS: 104 South Fifth Street    CITY: Spanish Lake   STATE:  MO

ZIP: 63137-2558    PHONE: 314-555-8702   CR LIMIT: $750.00   CR RATING: B


ACCOUNT #: 3045            NAME: Dr. Tony V. Estrella

INDEXED NAME: _____

ADDRESS: 401 Giles Road         CITY: Jennings    STATE:  MO

ZIP: 63136-0825    PHONE: 314-555-3171   CR LIMIT: $1500.00 CR RATING: B


ACCOUNT #: 3046            NAME: Beth-Anne G. Harper

INDEXED NAME: _____

ADDRESS: Route 2, Box 156       CITY: Spanish Lake   STATE:  MO

ZIP: 63137-0989    PHONE: 314-555-0830   CR LIMIT: $1250.00 CR RATING: B


ACCOUNT #: 3047            NAME: Stephen L. Wallenstein

INDEXED NAME: _____

ADDRESS: 1009 Ascot Lane       CITY: St. Louis   STATE:  MO

ZIP: 63106-5410    PHONE: 314-555-8275   CR LIMIT: $500.00  CR RATING: C

## PROJECT THREE | Jacobsen's Department Store

## Assignment 18: Locate Information in the Database Using Filters

You have received requests from the sales manager for the following information about credit customers. These questions can be answered quickly from the AccountInfo form using the Filter by Form button.

Open the Project Three database and click on the tab that says FORMS. Click on the form named AccountInfo and click Open. Click on the Filter by Form icon on the toolbar: ( ). The form should change to show all blank fields. Fill in the appropriate field with the item you are to look for. Access has an autofill feature that fills in the field with the first matching item. For example, you may need to type only *Dani* in the Name field for the form to locate the record for Daniel P. Schlotzhauer. Press the Tab key on your keyboard once the correct item has filled in.

Click on the Filter icon ( ) on the toolbar to show the complete record(s). If there is more than one record, the record navigator will show how many records there are. When you have written the information you need, click the Filter icon ( ) again to turn the filtering off.

Repeat this procedure for each information request. Remember to remove previous filter items by selecting the entire field and pressing the Backspace or Delete key on your keyboard. (A blank field means that the field is not considered when filtering.)

1. Name of customer with account number 1073.

   1. _____

2. Phone number of account number 2652.

   2. _____

3. Credit limit of Daniel P. Schlotzhauer.

   3. _____

4. Phone number of Diego H. Vaccarezza.

   4. _____

5. Street address of Lora-Lee Kelley.

   5. _____

6. Credit limit and credit rating of account number 2195.

   6. _____

7. Name of customer whose phone number is 314-555-8639.

   7. _____

8. Account number of Denise J. Schuster.

   8. _____

**9.** Name and full address of account number 2237.

_____

_____

**10.** Credit rating of Barry D. Lawson.                      **10.** _____

**11.** Account number and name of customer whose
address is P.O. Box 909, Spanish Lake, MO.        **11.** _____

_____

Jacobsen's
Department Store

## Assignment 19: Retrieve Information from the Customer Table Using Queries

Another of your job responsibilities is to query the customer table for information about specific groups of customers. Each of the questions below represents a request about groups of customers. You should create a query to generate a set of records that satisfies the criteria in the question. Follow instructions provided by your instructor to create queries that answer the following questions.

1. How many customers have a credit rating of C?

1. _____

2. How many customers have a credit limit of more than $1500? (Do not include customers whose credit limit is exactly $1500.)

2. _____

3. What are the names and phone numbers of all customers who live in St. Charles?

| Name | Phone |
|------|-------|
| _____ | _____ |
| _____ | _____ |
| _____ | _____ |
| _____ | _____ |
| _____ | _____ |
| _____ | _____ |

4. How many customers live in Illinois?

4. _____

**5.** What are the account numbers and names of all customers whose last names begin with the letter F?

| Account # | Name |
|-----------|------|
|           |      |
|           |      |
|           |      |
|           |      |
|           |      |
|           |      |
|           |      |

**6.** How many customers have a credit rating of B *and* a credit limit of exactly $1000?

6. _____

**7.** What are the names of the customers who live in St. Louis and have a credit limit of $1750?

| Name | |
|------|---|
|      |   |
|      |   |

**8.** What are the names and phone numbers of customers whose last names begin with the letters G, H, and I *and* who have a credit rating of A?

| Name | Phone |
|------|-------|
|      |       |
|      |       |
|      |       |
|      |       |
|      |       |

**9.** How many customers live in Florissant and have a credit rating of B?

9. _____

**10.** How many customers who live in Missouri have a credit limit less than $750? (Do not count those whose credit limit is exactly $750.)

10. _____

**PROJECT THREE**

# Jacobsen's Department Store

## Assignment 20: Print Customer Information

The customer database is used by Jacobsen's Department Store for many applications. One important use is the creation of printed reports, lists, and labels. In this assignment you will use the customer table to produce queries that will be used, in turn, to generate reports in response to requests for printed information. After completing each task, answer the question related to it in the space provided.

1. Print a mailing label for each customer who lives in Alton, IL. Each label should include data from the following fields: *Name, Address, City, State,* and *Zip.*

    **Q:** How many labels did you print?        1. _____

2. Print a list of the account numbers, names, and credit limits of all customers with account numbers less than 1000. Print the list in ascending order by account number. Use the report designer to modify column headings and thus make the report presentable to your supervisors.

    **Q:** How many customers are on the list?        2. _____

3. Print an alphabetical list of the names and phone numbers of customers who live in Ferguson, MO. *Hint:* You may want to do the sort on the IndexedName field but print the name from the Name field.

    **Q:** How many customers are on the list?        3. _____

Name _____Date_____Score _____

# Jacobsen's Department Store

## Assignment 21: Project Quiz

Before you take this quiz, you should have completed the previous assignments so that your customer database contains all changes, queries, and reports.

1. How many fields are in the Customer table?

   1. _____

2. What is the phone number of the customer number whose account number is 0882? Change the phone number of this customer to 314-555-4917.

   2. _____

3. What is the name of the customer whose account number is 1048? Delete the record.

   3. _____

4. Add a record to the Customer table using the following information. Write the indexed name in the space provided.

   ACCOUNT #: 3048

   NAME: Reva G. Shane-Lewis

   INDEXED NAME:

   4. _____

   ADDRESS: 318 Darlington Ave.

   CITY: Spanish Lake

   STATE: MO

   ZIP: 63137-1250

   PHONE: 314-555-2132

   CREDIT LIMIT: $750.00

   CREDIT RATING: B

5. What are the credit limit and credit rating of the customer whose account number is 2290?

   5. _____

6. What is the phone number of Heather A. Winkler?

   6. _____

7. How many customers live in Edwardsville?

   7. _____

**8.** List the names of all customers who live in Illinois *and* have a credit rating of C.

**Name**

_____     _____

_____     _____

**9.** List the names of all customers who have a credit limit less than $750 (do not include those whose credit limit is exactly $750) *and* a credit rating of C.

**Name**

_____     _____

_____     _____

_____     _____

_____     _____

_____     _____

_____     _____

_____     _____

_____     _____

**10.** Print a mailing label for each customer living in Spanish Lake whose last name begins with the letter S. How many labels did you print?

10. _____

Name _____ Date_____ Score ____

# New Age Office Supply

## Assignment 22: Document the New Age Database Table Design

Follow your instructor's directions and install the database on your lab computer. Open the database and click on the tab that says TABLES. Click on the required table and click on Design ( ). You can now view the names and types of each field in the current table. Click on each field and get the Field Size. Some text fields use an Input Mask to force the data to look a certain way. For example, if you input a zip code, you always want it to look like 23456-9999, with the dash between the fifth and sixth numbers. Adding an Input Mask will format the zip codes as you want them to appear and will also allow the operator to type in the zip code without the dash, increasing efficiency. If the field is a Text type field, indicate under *Mask* whether or not a mask is used.

What are the names of the tables and fields? (The first field is given as an example.)

**Table Name:** _Customer_ _____

| **Field Name** | **Type** | **Size** | **Mask?** |
|---|---|---|---|
| _Customer ID_ | _Number_ | _Long Integer_ | _No_ |
| | | | |
| | | | |
| | | | |
| | | | |
| | | | |
| | | | |
| | | | |

**Note:** The Customer table contains a numeric field called StateID. When you open the table and view the data, a two-letter state abbreviation with a field name of State will display. In Design Mode, click on StateID. Under field proper you will see Caption contains State. Click the Lookup tab. On the Row Source line is a Select statement. Click in line and then click on the elipsis button ( ). You will see that the StateID field in this table is related to the StateID field in the StateTax table. The two-letter state abbreviation is actually retrieved from the StateTax table.

**Table Name:** _____

| **Field Name** | **Type** | **Size** | **Mask?** |
| --- | --- | --- | --- |
| _____ | _____ | _____ | _____ |
| _____ | _____ | _____ | _____ |
| _____ | _____ | _____ | _____ |
| _____ | _____ | _____ | _____ |
| _____ | _____ | _____ | _____ |
| _____ | _____ | _____ | _____ |
| _____ | _____ | _____ | _____ |
| _____ | _____ | _____ | _____ |
| _____ | _____ | _____ | _____ |

**Table Name:** _____

| **Field Name** | **Type** | **Size** | **Mask?** |
| --- | --- | --- | --- |
| _____ | _____ | _____ | _____ |
| _____ | _____ | _____ | _____ |
| _____ | _____ | _____ | _____ |
| _____ | _____ | _____ | _____ |
| _____ | _____ | _____ | _____ |
| _____ | _____ | _____ | _____ |
| _____ | _____ | _____ | _____ |
| _____ | _____ | _____ | _____ |
| _____ | _____ | _____ | _____ |

**Note:** The Inventory table has a SupplierID field which is numeric, but when you open the Inventory table in Display mode, you can see the supplier's name. Why does this happen? (*Hint:* See the explanation on page 105 for StateID Customer table.)

**Table Name:** _____

| **Field Name** | **Type** | **Size** | **Mask?** |
| --- | --- | --- | --- |
| _____ | _____ | _____ | _____ |
| _____ | _____ | _____ | _____ |
| _____ | _____ | _____ | _____ |
| _____ | _____ | _____ | _____ |
| _____ | _____ | _____ | _____ |
| _____ | _____ | _____ | _____ |
| _____ | _____ | _____ | _____ |
| _____ | _____ | _____ | _____ |
| _____ | _____ | _____ | _____ |

**Table Name:** _____

| **Field Name** | **Type** | **Size** | **Mask?** |
| --- | --- | --- | --- |
| _____ | _____ | _____ | _____ |
| _____ | _____ | _____ | _____ |
| _____ | _____ | _____ | _____ |
| _____ | _____ | _____ | _____ |
| _____ | _____ | _____ | _____ |
| _____ | _____ | _____ | _____ |
| _____ | _____ | _____ | _____ |
| _____ | _____ | _____ | _____ |
| _____ | _____ | _____ | _____ |
| _____ | _____ | _____ | _____ |

**Table Name:** _____

| **Field Name** | **Type** | **Size** | **Mask?** |
| --- | --- | --- | --- |
| _____ | _____ | _____ | _____ |
| _____ | _____ | _____ | _____ |
| _____ | _____ | _____ | _____ |
| _____ | _____ | _____ | _____ |
| _____ | _____ | _____ | _____ |
| _____ | _____ | _____ | _____ |
| _____ | _____ | _____ | _____ |
| _____ | _____ | _____ | _____ |
| _____ | _____ | _____ | _____ |
| _____ | _____ | _____ | _____ |
| _____ | _____ | _____ | _____ |

**Table Name:** _____

| **Field Name** | **Type** | **Size** | **Mask?** |
| --- | --- | --- | --- |
| _____ | _____ | _____ | _____ |
| _____ | _____ | _____ | _____ |
| _____ | _____ | _____ | _____ |
| _____ | _____ | _____ | _____ |
| _____ | _____ | _____ | _____ |
| _____ | _____ | _____ | _____ |
| _____ | _____ | _____ | _____ |
| _____ | _____ | _____ | _____ |
| _____ | _____ | _____ | _____ |
| _____ | _____ | _____ | _____ |
| _____ | _____ | _____ | _____ |
| _____ | _____ | _____ | _____ |

**Table Name:** _____

**Field Name**      **Type**      **Size**      **Mask?**

_____  _____  _____  _____

_____  _____  _____  _____

_____  _____  _____  _____

_____  _____  _____  _____

_____  _____  _____  _____

_____  _____  _____  _____

_____  _____  _____  _____

_____  _____  _____  _____

_____  _____  _____  _____

_____  _____  _____  _____


**Table Name:** _____

**Field Name**      **Type**      **Size**      **Mask?**

_____  _____  _____  _____

_____  _____  _____  _____

_____  _____  _____  _____

_____  _____  _____  _____

_____  _____  _____  _____

_____  _____  _____  _____

_____  _____  _____  _____

_____  _____  _____  _____

_____  _____  _____  _____

_____  _____  _____  _____

## PROJECT FOUR

# New Age
# Office Supply

## Assignment 23: Explore the New Age Database Table Design

Open the Project Four database and click on the tab that says TABLES.

1. The Description field of the Inventory table contains a brief description of each product. What is the description of the product with ProductCode E3-0258?

   1. _____

2. The number of items in stock for each product is entered in the NoOnHand field of the Inventory table. This number is decreased when sales are recorded, and it is increased when products are received. How many items of Product Code A3-0256 are on hand?

   2. _____

3. The UnitCost field in the Inventory table shows the amount paid by New Age Office Supply for each product. These amounts change periodically as suppliers raise and lower their prices. What is the cost for Product Code B1-0216?

   3. _____

4. The amount charged by New Age Office Supply for each product has been entered in the SellingPrice field of the Inventory table. This amount is based on several factors, including unit cost and sales volume. What is the selling price of the product you found in question 3 above?

   4. _____

5. The difference between the unit cost and the selling price is called the *gross margin*. This amount is the profit made on a product before counting the expense of doing business. Figure the gross margin for Product Code B1-0216 (see questions 3 and 4 above).

   5. _____

6. There are three types of customers that frequent New Age Office Supply: individuals, businesses, and government organizations. The database keeps track of this difference so that New Age can send the proper types of advertising to each customer. What type of customer is Harvey Ramirez, Ph.D.?

   6. _____

7. The database tables store information that allows New Age Office Supply to maintain its inventory, its customer information, and all product sales in one database. Each table contains information about one or more aspects of the business. Which table contains only information related to the store's customers?

7. _____

8. Which table contains information related to the sale of individual inventory products?

8. _____

9. A customer will often buy more than one item when visiting the store. Which table holds information about store visits?

9. _____

10. Special tables, called *Bridge tables,* connect records from two or more tables together in a "many-to-many" relationship. These tables usually contain only numbers that are keys in other tables. What table acts as a bridge between the SalesTicket table and the Inventory table?

10. _____

## PROJECT FOUR

# New Age
# Office Supply

## Assignment 24: Explore the Relationships in the New Age Database

Open the Project Four database and click the Relationships button ( ▣ ) on the main tool-bar. The Relationships window will appear. Each block in the window represents one of the tables in the database. Lines connecting the table blocks represent a relationship be-tween those tables. The line connects the related field in one table to its counterpart in related tables. This arrangement indicates that the fields contain the same information. For example, the Customer table and the StateTax table are related. The relationship is between the StateID field of the Customer table and the StateID field of the StateTax table.

1. Name all related tables in the database in the space below. Write only the names of the tables. The order of the tables does not matter, and some tables may appear more than once. The first relation is provided as a guide.

<u>   *Customer*   </u>    is related to    <u>   *StateTax*   </u>

<u>            </u>    is related to    <u>            </u>

<u>            </u>    is related to    <u>            </u>

<u>            </u>    is related to    <u>            </u>

<u>            </u>    is related to    <u>            </u>

2. In any relationship, one of the two related fields is a key field for the table containing it. The relationship connection often has a 1 field and a Many ($\infty$) field. The 1 field is a key in its table because there will be only one occurrence of a particular value of that field. For each of the following tables, enter the field that is a key field.

| Table Name | Key Field |
|------------|-----------|
| Customer | _____ |
| SalesTicket | _____ |
| StateTax | _____ |
| Inventory | _____ |
| Suppliers | _____ |

3. The roles of many databases change as they are used. Occasionally, a new table will need to be added to the existing database. This database has just had new tables added so products can be added to the database quickly. You will need to create relationships between existing tables and the new tables. When new tables are created, they are not automatically visible in the Relationships window. Make the ReceiptItem table, ReceivingTicket table, and the Employee table visible in the window by following these steps:

- Right-click in the window.
- Choose *Show Table.* . . .
- Click on the desired table and click the Add button.
- Add the tables, then click *Close*.

4. The new tables do not have any relationships set. Set up the following relationships and indicate completion by signing your name in the space provided. Put a check mark in the Referential Integrity box of the Relationships configuration window.

| **Relationship** | **Confirmation** |
| --- | --- |
| InventoryID in SalesItem is related to ProductCode in Inventory | _____ |
| SalesTicketID in SalesTicket is related to SalesTicketID in SalesItem | _____ |
| EmployeeID in SalesTicket is related to EmployeeID in Employee | _____ |

## PROJECT FOUR

# New Age
# Office Supply

## Assignment 25: Delete Inventory Items from the New Age Database

Open the database and click on the tab that says TABLES. Open the Inventory table by double-clicking on Inventory (or click on Inventory and click the Open button.)

New Age Office Supply needs to remove from its database products that are no longer carried or manufactured. Use the information below and delete the records from the Inventory table. Document the deletions by initialing the item in the space provided.

1. PRODUCTCODE: B3-0344
   DESCRIPTION: DATA CART

   1. _____

2. PRODUCTCODE: B3-0398
   DESCRIPTION: MOBILE SECURITY CABINET

   2. _____

3. PRODUCTCODE: D2-0453
   DESCRIPTION: VISIBLE FILE 10 TRAY

   3. _____

4. PRODUCTCODE: E3-0237
   DESCRIPTION: MAG TAPE CARRYING CASE

   4. _____

5. PRODUCTCODE: G4-0344
   DESCRIPTION: STANDING DIRECTORY BOARD

   5. _____

# PROJECT FOUR · New Age Office Supply

## Assignment 26: Add Inventory Items to the New Age Database

New Age Office Supply frequently adds new items to its product line. The forms below contain information about ten new products for which there are no former NoOnHand amounts. Your entry in the NoOnHand field of the database will be the number received.

Open the Project Four database and click on the FORMS tab. Double-click on the Inventory form. Click on the New Record button on the navigation bar to start adding the new records. Be sure to fill in each of the fields except the InventoryValue field. Calculate the Inventory Value by multiplying UnitCost by NoInStock. Record the result in the space provided in each form below.

PRODUCTCODE: A1-0194      DESCRIPTION: MICROCOMPUTER CENTER
SUPPLIER: Data Case Enterprises
UNITCOST: $94.50      SELLINGPRICE: $175.00      NO. RECEIVED: 6
INVENTORYVALUE: _____

PRODUCTCODE: B1-0127      DESCRIPTION: ROLLING FILE
SUPPLIER: Steel Furniture Company
UNITCOST: $83.50      SELLINGPRICE: $144.00      NO. RECEIVED: 4
INVENTORYVALUE: _____

PRODUCTCODE: B3-0327      DESCRIPTION: MOBILE DATA UNIT
SUPPLIER: DCR Business Equipment
UNITCOST: $80.60      SELLINGPRICE: $139.00      NO. RECEIVED: 12
INVENTORYVALUE: _____

PRODUCTCODE: D2-0488      DESCRIPTION: PORTABLE VISIBLE FILE
SUPPLIER: Torrence File Products
UNITCOST: $51.90      SELLINGPRICE: $92.80      NO. RECEIVED: 24
INVENTORYVALUE: _____

PRODUCTCODE: E1-0289      DESCRIPTION: CONTINENTAL ATTACHE
SUPPLIER: United Luggage
UNITCOST: $39.00      SELLINGPRICE: $75.00      NO. RECEIVED: 12
INVENTORYVALUE: _____

PRODUCTCODE: E2-0411     DESCRIPTION: EASY OPEN PORTFOLIO
SUPPLIER: Fancini Products
UNITCOST: $8.10          SELLINGPRICE: $15.50        NO. RECEIVED: 36
INVENTORYVALUE: _____


PRODUCTCODE: F1-0147     DESCRIPTION: COMPACT DISK STAPLER
SUPPLIER: Romereo Manufacturing Co.
UNITCOST: $5.90          SELLINGPRICE: $8.95         NO. RECEIVED: 60
INVENTORYVALUE: _____


PRODUCTCODE: G4-0242     DESCRIPTION: TELESCOPING POINTER
SUPPLIER: Romereo Manufacturing Co.
UNITCOST: $2.10          SELLINGPRICE: $3.50         NO. RECEIVED: 24
INVENTORYVALUE: _____


PRODUCTCODE: H1-0323     DESCRIPTION: DESK ORGANIZER
SUPPLIER: Quality Office Systems
UNITCOST: $3.05          SELLINGPRICE: $5.50         NO. RECEIVED: 60
INVENTORYVALUE: _____


PRODUCTCODE: H4-0150     DESCRIPTION: PAPER SHREDDER
SUPPLIER: Superior Office Products
UNITCOST: $304.95        SELLINGPRICE: $449.00       NO. RECEIVED: 2
INVENTORYVALUE: _____

| PROJECT FOUR | New Age Office Supply |
|---|---|

## Assignment 27: Add Sales to the New Age Database

Open the database and click on the tab that says FORMS. You will see that there are four forms named; however, all the forms were created as part of the SalesTicket form, which you will use here. The sales ticket allows a person at the cash register or telephone to enter the complete sales information for any existing customers.

Double-click on the SalesTicket form (or click once and click the Open button) to open the form. DO NOT ATTEMPT TO OPEN ANY OTHER FORM. There are five areas in the sales ticket:

- The top section shows the name of the business (New Age Office Supply) and the salesperson.

- Next is an area for the date and time of sale and the customer information. Selecting or typing in the name of a current customer automatically brings up his or her address information.

- The next area shows a list of items purchased by the customer. Each row of the list is one inventory item.

- The area below the detailed list shows the total information. It also provides a means for adding a new item to the sales ticket.

- Last is the record navigation that allows the salesperson to move from one ticket to another.

To add a new sale to customer information that exists in the database:

- Click on the New Record button in the navigation area at the bottom of the screen. Record: |◄ ◄ | 1 | ► ►| ►* | of 30

- Select the customer by using the drop-down list.

- Select the salesperson.

- In the "Detail" area, add the sale(s) by selecting either the ProductCode or the Description in the first blank line. Use the tab key on your keyboard to move from field to field.

Add the following sales into the Sales Ticket form. Confirm the entry by writing down the total charge for the order.

| NAME: | Harvey Ramirez, Ph.D. | | DATE: | 4/7/02 |
|---|---|---|---|---|
| ADDRESS: | 341 Meadowdale Blvd. | | TIME: | 11:45:00 AM |
| | Spanish Lake, MO 63137-1466 | | | |

| ProductCode | Description | Quantity | SellingPrice | ItemTotal |
|---|---|---|---|---|
| A1-0233 | BI-LEVEL COMPUTER STAND | 2 | $155.00 | $310.00 |
| B1-0206 | 3 DRAWER FILE, LEGAL | 3 | $239.00 | $717.00 |
| H1-0348 | BOOKENDS | 6 | $11.98 | $71.88 |
| | | | **Total** | _____ |

| NAME: | BBQ2 Sports Bar | | DATE: | 4/7/02 |
|---|---|---|---|---|
| ADDRESS: | 2345 Bell Ave | | TIME: | 10:24:58 PM |
| | Granite City, IL 62040-1235 | | | |

| ProductCode | Description | Quantity | SellingPrice | ItemTotal |
|---|---|---|---|---|
| B2-0184 | 3 DRAWER LATERAL FILE | 2 | $537.95 | $1,075.90 |
| E2-0543 | BUDGET PORTFOLIO | 1 | $19.40 | $19.40 |
| | | | **Total** | _____ |

| NAME: | Charles G. Zehmer, III | | DATE: | 4/8/02 |
|---|---|---|---|---|
| ADDRESS: | 16 Westbrook Avenue | | TIME: | 3:28:26 PM |
| | Spanish Lake, MO 63137-0442 | | | |

| ProductCode | Description | Quantity | SellingPrice | ItemTotal |
|---|---|---|---|---|
| A1-0233 | BI-LEVEL COMPUTER STAND | 1 | $155.00 | $155.00 |
| A4-0488 | SLED BASE STACKING CHAIR | 10 | $87.70 | $877.00 |
| | | | **Total** | _____ |

| NAME: | Fun-n-Games Hobby Shop | | DATE: | 4/8/02 |
|---|---|---|---|---|
| ADDRESS: | 2355 Bell Ave | | TIME: | 3:52:21 PM |
| | Granite City, IL 62040-1245 | | | |

| ProductCode | Description | Quantity | SellingPrice | ItemTotal |
|---|---|---|---|---|
| A1-0233 | BI-LEVEL COMPUTER STAND | 1 | $155.00 | $155.00 |
| B1-0166 | 5 DRAWER FILE, LEGAL | 2 | $363.00 | $726.00 |
| E3-0174 | EXPANDING ENVELOPE | 5 | $9.15 | $45.75 |
| | | | **Total** | _____ |

| NAME: | Scott R. Taulbee | | DATE: | 4/8/02 |
|---|---|---|---|---|
| ADDRESS: | Route 2, Box 192 | | TIME: | 5:41:00 PM |
| | Spanish Lake, MO 63137-0625 | | | |

| ProductCode | Description | Quantity | SellingPrice | ItemTotal |
|---|---|---|---|---|
| F2-0213 | 2-HOLE ECONOMY PUNCH | 1 | $8.45 | $8.45 |
| H2-0275 | ASYMMETRIC LAMP | 1 | $89.00 | $89.00 |
| | | | **Total** | _____ |

| NAME: | Mary E. Babbitt | | DATE: | 4/8/02 |
| ADDRESS: | 316 Cedar Creek Lane | | TIME: | 5:42:30 PM |
| | Granite City, IL 62040-1466 | | | |

| ProductCode | Description | Quantity | SellingPrice | ItemTotal |
|---|---|---|---|---|
| B3-0379 | 4 WAY DATA RACK | 1 | $204.50 | $204.50 |
| D1-0124 | BUSINESS CARD FILE | 2 | $17.95 | $35.90 |
| | | | **Total** _____ | |

| NAME: | Children's Garden | | DATE: | 4/8/02 |
| ADDRESS: | 3455 Klosterman Drive | | TIME: | 5:47:32 PM |
| | St. Louis, MO 63136-0744 | | | |

| ProductCode | Description | Quantity | SellingPrice | ItemTotal |
|---|---|---|---|---|
| D1-0124 | BUSINESS CARD FILE | 2 | $17.95 | $35.90 |
| E2-0543 | BUDGET PORTFOLIO | 5 | $19.40 | $97.00 |
| | | | **Total** _____ | |

| NAME: | Scott R. Taulbee | | DATE: | 4/8/02 |
| ADDRESS: | Route 2, Box 192 | | TIME: | 6:06:26 PM |
| | Spanish Lake, MO 63137-0625 | | | |

| ProductCode | Description | Quantity | SellingPrice | ItemTotal |
|---|---|---|---|---|
| C2-0235 | CASH BOX | 1 | $38.95 | $38.95 |
| D1-0212 | COVERED VUE FILE | 1 | $24.75 | $24.75 |
| H2-0245 | CLAMP-ON EXTENSION LAMP | 1 | $46.00 | $46.00 |
| | | | **Total** _____ | |

| NAME: | Linda R. McDonald | | DATE: | 4/8/02 |
| ADDRESS: | 212 Elm Street | | TIME: | 6:12:59 PM |
| | Spanish Lake, MO 63137-0435 | | | |

| ProductCode | Description | Quantity | SellingPrice | ItemTotal |
|---|---|---|---|---|
| D1-0274 | ROTARY CARD FILE 3 x 5 | 1 | $32.95 | $32.95 |
| F1-0332 | ELECTRIC STAPLER | 1 | $124.95 | $124.95 |
| G3-0189 | MONTHLY PLANNER | 1 | $63.00 | $63.00 |
| | | | **Total** _____ | |

| NAME: | Caroline Hostetter | | DATE: | 4/8/02 |
| ADDRESS: | 105 Marina Circle | | TIME: | 6:14:10 PM |
| | St. Louis, MO 63114-6328 | | | |

| ProductCode | Description | Quantity | SellingPrice | ItemTotal |
|---|---|---|---|---|
| A3-0525 | SIDE CHAIR | 1 | $299.75 | $299.75 |
| | | | **Total** _____ | |

Name _____ Date_____Score ____

**PROJECT FOUR**

# New Age
# Office Supply

## Assignment 28: Create a New Form for Suppliers in the New Age Database

Databases are always evolving. When New Age constructed the database, suppliers data were relatively constant. The occasional change to the Suppliers table was accomplished by adding the information directly to the table.

As the store grows, however, the suppliers change more regularly. Your boss has asked you to allow suppliers to be added or changed using a user-friendly form instead of using the table. Open the database and click on the tab that says FORMS.

1. Click on the *New* button to begin creating the Supplier's form.

2. Choose the option called Form Wizard. This option will take you through the steps for creating a new form.

3. Below the wizard selection is a drop-down list that lets you choose a table or query from which to retrieve information to put in the form. Choose the Suppliers table and click the OK button.

4. You are now presented with a list of fields from the Suppliers table that you can use in your form. Click on the ⟫ button to move all the fields into the area that says Selected Fields, then click the Next button.

5. You will now be presented with options for the design of your form. You are creating this form as a way to enter information about new suppliers or to change current information. You want to see only one supplier at a time. The two choices that will give one supplier on each screen are Columnar and Justified. Choose the option that best suits your taste and record your choice here.     5. _____

6. Click on *Next*.

7. You are now given a choice of background and control styles. Clicking on each style shows a preview of what the final form will look like in the area to the left of the wizard. Choose a style that best suits your taste and record your choice. Click on *Next*.     7. _____

8. The only remaining item is the name of the form. Access will name it for you, but you can change the name to something else if you like. Record the name of the form here.     8. _____

9. Choose the View or Enter Information option, and click Finish.

10. You can now use the navigation controls at the bottom of the screen to scroll from supplier to supplier. You can also add new suppliers by clicking on the New Record button in the navigation area.

| PROJECT FOUR | New Age Office Supply |
|---|---|

## Assignment 29: Create a Query that Lists Sales for the Last Month

Now that the New Age database has sales entered, you will want to view them. You can build a report that shows all the sales. After a period of time, however, the report will be tens or hundreds of pages long.

The accounting manager at New Age Office Supply wants a summary of all sales for the current month. You will have to build a query that retrieves the information from the necessary tables and sets a criterion that lists only sales for the month.

1. Click on the Queries tab in the Database window. Click the New button.

2. Because you will be displaying information from more than one table, you need to design the query from scratch. Click on the Design View option and click the OK button.

3. Next, a blank query builder window and a selector appear. They show each of the tables or other queries that you will use to obtain information. You will use fields from the Employee table, Customer table, and SalesTicket table. For each, click on the table name in the window, then click on the Add button. When all three tables are shown in the top part of the query builder, click on the Close button.

4. Check that all the required relationships are visible. EmployeeID in the Employee and SalesTicket tables should be related, and CustomerID in the SalesTicket and Customer tables should also be related.

5. You now need to select the fields you want displayed by the query. Select a field, then drag it to one of the columns in the lower half of the query builder on the row labeled Field. A field icon [ Solo ] will appear. When you have the location correct, release the mouse button to add the field. Add the following fields to the query. Verify your work by writing your initials in the space provided.

| Table Name | Field Name | Initials |
|---|---|---|
| Employee | EmployeeName | _____ |
| SalesTicket | Date | _____ |
| Customer | CustomerName | _____ |
| Customer | ZipCode | _____ |
| SalesTicket | Subtotal | _____ |
| SalesTicket | Tax | _____ |
| SalesTicket | Total | _____ |

6. Now that you have all of your fields selected, you need to reduce the total number of records produced by the query by setting a criteria.

  - Set the cursor on the line marked Criteria in the column that contains the Date field.

  - Type the line listed below. After you have typed the line, replace the dates in this line with the date from approximately a month ago and today's date.

$$>=\#3/1/2002\#\ \text{AND}\ <=\#4/5/2002\#$$

  The line, as it is typed here, indicates that if the Date is on or after March 1, 2002 *and* it is on or before April 5, 2002, the criteria are satisfied and the record will be displayed.

  **Note:** The # signs before and after the date indicate that the number within should be interpreted as a date. Otherwise, Access will think you are asking to calculate the equation $3 \div 1 \div 2002$.

7. Now you are ready to run the query. If you have added the sales from Assignment 27 during the last month, you can generate a list by running the query with the ▮ button on the toolbar.

8. Finally, save the query. Click on the Close control in the Query window, or click the Save button on the toolbar. When the Name window appears, name the query SalesForMonth.

| PROJECT FOUR | New Age Office Supply |
|---|---|

## Assignment 30: Create a Printable Report of Monthly Sales

The query you created in Assignment 29 will be used to create an *Access* report of the sales for the previous month. Because queries give only raw numbers and because forms are meant for interactive viewing on the computer screen, you need to build a report that will obtain information from the database and format it so that it can be printed and presented to a manager or sent through the mail.

1.  Open the database and click on the Reports tab. Click the New button.

2.  Like the form you constructed in Assignment 28, you will use the wizard to guide your creation of the sales report. Choose the Report Wizard.

3.  The report will take information from the query you built in Assignment 29. Use the drop-down list below the wizard to choose SalesForMonth, which is the query from the previous assignment. Click *Next*.

4.  Use the ⟩⟩ button to move all the fields into the Selected Fields area and click the Next button.

5.  You can now choose how to group the printouts. This window allows you to sort by date. Click the option that says *by Sales Ticket*. Click the Next button.

6.  The next window gives you the option of grouping by individual fields. Click the Date field and click the ⟩ button. Next, click on the EmployeeName field and click the ⟩ button. These choices will provide two levels of grouping when you produce your printout. Click the Next button.

7.  In the most detailed area, you will want to sort sales by the time of day and day of the month, so choose *Date* from the drop-down list next to the *1* label.

8.  Before continuing, you will want to sum the sales for each group; click on the button marked *Summary Options*.

9.  In the Summary Options window, click the box in the Sum column for each item (Subtotal, Tax, and Total). Also click in the check box marked *Calculate percentage of total for sums*. You will want to see all the transactions, so leave the Detail and Summary option checked. Click the OK button. Then click the Next button.

10. Choose a layout option and an orientation for your printout. Record your choices here:

    Layout: _____

    Orientation: _____

    Click the "Next" button.

**11.** Choose a report style. Record your choice. _____

Click the Next button. _____

**12.** Name your report SalesByMonth. Click on the Finish button to view your final report. Print the report and present it to your instructor.

**Note:** You may wish to change the sizes and locations of some of the fields. To do so, click on the Design Mode () button on the toolbar and make changes. Return to the Preview Mode () by clicking on that button (located at the same place) on the toolbar.

| PROJECT FOUR | New Age Office Supply |
|---|---|

## Assignment 31: Create a Printable Report of Inventory

You have been approached by the receiving clerk with a request for information about what is in stock. Specifically, you are asked to list all the products by supplier. To expedite reordering, you are requested to include the contact information for each supplier. This request will require creating a report from two different tables: the Inventory table and the Suppliers table. You don't need a query here because you are not limiting the amount of information that goes into the report; you want to print out everything in stock.

1. Open the database and click on the Reports tab. Click the New button.

2. Choose the Report Wizard. Click the OK button.

3. You will need to choose fields from two tables. For each item below, choose the table from the drop-down list. Then choose the appropriate field, and click on the Next ⟩ button to move it into the Selected Fields area. Verify your work by writing your initials in the space provided.

| Table Name | Field Name | Initials |
|---|---|---|
| Suppliers | SupplierName | _____ |
| Suppliers | StreetAddress | _____ |
| Suppliers | City | _____ |
| Suppliers | State | _____ |
| Suppliers | ZipCode | _____ |
| Suppliers | PhoneNo | _____ |
| Suppliers | FaxNo | _____ |
| Suppliers | CustomerNo | _____ |
| Inventory | ProductCode | _____ |
| Inventory | Description | _____ |
| Inventory | UnitCost | _____ |
| Inventory | NoOnHand | _____ |

When you are finished, click the "Next" button.

4. You want to group the items in your report by supplier, so choose *by Suppliers* and click the Next button.

5. You are now given the choice of creating more defined groups by choosing individual fields for grouping. For example, if one supplier had several addresses, you might want to use the supplier's name to group the addresses. However, you do not want to choose this option now. Do not choose any fields for grouping. Click the Next button.

6. You can sort the individual items by the Description field. Choose that field from the drop-down list by the *1* label. Then click on *Summary Options*.

7. You will sum only the number of products in stock. Click the check box in the Sum column for NoOnHand. Click the OK button. Then click the Next button in the Sorting window.

8. Choose a layout option and an orientation for your printout. Record your choices here:

   Layout: _____

   Orientation: _____

   Click the Next button.

9. Choose a report style. Record your choice here: _____

   Click the Next button.

10. Name your report *InventoryReport*. Click on the Finish button to view your final report.

**11.** You will notice that the report does not look appealing. Click on the Design button on the toolbar to move items around. Hints for redesign are listed below.

- Each level of grouping is in an area in the Design window. You can make headers for columns in the Detail area by creating labels with the Label ( **Aa** ) button in the Toolbox window and dragging out space in the SupplierIDHeader area.

- You can also copy labels that are located in the Page Header area and paste them in another area. Click on the label once to select it, drag over the text, and type new text for your new header. This option allows you to use the same format you used for the larger labels.

- You can use the Line( ![line button] ) button in the Toolbox window to create lines for separating the headers from the detail items in the finished report.

- If you wish to add white space to the Detail area or to one of the headers, place the cursor in the detail area bar at the bottom of the detail section area. When the cursor changes, drag it down to increase the size of the detail area.

**Note:** You cannot decrease the size if the border runs into a label or field. You will need to move the labels, fields, and lines before you can reduce the size further.

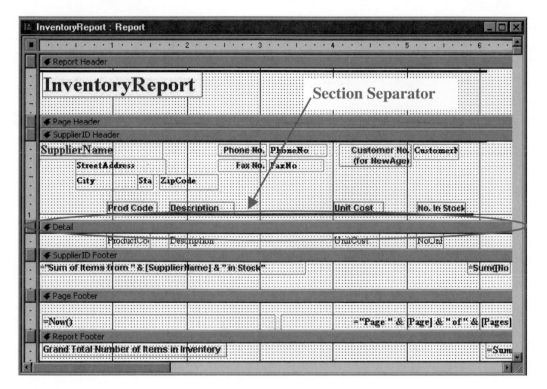

![PROJECT FOUR] **New Age Office Supply**

## Assignment 32: Project Quiz

Before you take this quiz, you should have completed the previous assignments so that your database contains all changes, queries, forms, and reports.

1. How many tables are in the New Age database?   1._____

2. How many fields are in the Inventory table?   2._____

3. In a query, what are the criteria for selecting only records with dates between March 1, 2001 and March 15, 2001?   3._____

4. What is the total amount due for the Sales Ticket with the CustomerID 891? (*Hint:* Use a table.)   4._____

5. What is the total amount due for the Sales Ticket for the customer named *Caroline Hostetter*? (*Hint:* Use a report.)   5._____

6. What is the key field of the ReceivingTicket table?   6._____

7. What is the tax rate for Rhode Island?   7._____

8. The InventoryID field in the SalesItem table is related to which field in which table?

   Field: _____

   Table: _____

9. What is the total tax paid for all purchases currently in the database? (*Hint:* Modify a query, then open a report.)   9._____

10. Create a query to find all items from the supplier Superior Office Products that are currently in stock. What is the number of records generated by the query?   10._____

## PROJECT FIVE — NighTech Restaurant

In the previous two projects, you worked with existing databases that had already been designed and established. This project is different because you will be given information that you need in order to design a new database.

The NighTech Restaurant is a new eating establishment that caters to computer professionals in Reston, Virginia. You have been hired as a consultant to assist the accountant in creating a database for maintaining employee information and payroll.

## Assignment 33: Review Requirements for the Employee Database

In this assignment, you will examine the information that must be stored and how each piece of information relates to the others. The restaurant manager hands you two forms that contain all the information that will be tracked.

---

**Employee Information Form**

Name: _____  SSN: _____

       LAST       FIRST    MIDDLE INITIAL

Date of Birth: _____

Address: _____

City: _____

State: _____  Zip Code: _____

Married/Single: _____

Home Phone No.: _____  Job Title: _____

Cell Phone No.: _____  Full/Part Time: _____

Hire Date: _____  Hourly Wage: _____

---

## Employee Work Schedule

Name: _____                SSN: _____

| Day of Week | Date | Start Time | End Time |
|-------------|------|------------|----------|
| Monday      |      |            |          |
| Tuesday     |      |            |          |
| Wednesday   |      |            |          |
| Thursday    |      |            |          |
| Friday      |      |            |          |
| Saturday    |      |            |          |
| Sunday      |      |            |          |

Each of the forms contains information about the employee. Of course, the accountant and the manager would like all the information to be stored together. You need to determine how to store the information. The following is a list of functions that management would like the database to perform.

- Add new employees.

- Create schedules for each employee.

- Clock any employee in or out from one screen. The screen should show workshifts only for the current day.

- Print schedules for employees. The schedule should have the employee's name, social security number (SSN), and phone numbers at the top of the form so that the manager can also have a copy.

- Print a summary of times worked for each employee. The summary should show all times the employee worked during the month and should calculate the gross pay for that time. It should also total the hours and pay for the month.

Using the forms shown at the beginning of this assignment and the above requirements as a guide, provide the following information.

1. How many tables will be used in the database?            1. _____

2. What are the names of these tables? What general information will they contain?

| **Table Name** | **What Will Be in the Table (in General Terms)?** |
|----------------|---------------------------------------------------|
| _____ | _____ |
|                | _____ |
|                | _____ |

| **Table Name** | **What Will Be in the Table (in General Terms)?** |
|---|---|
| _____ | _____ |
| | _____ |
| | _____ |
| _____ | _____ |
| | _____ |
| | _____ |
| _____ | _____ |
| | _____ |
| | _____ |
| _____ | _____ |
| | _____ |
| | _____ |
| _____ | _____ |
| | _____ |
| | _____ |

**3.** How many queries will you need to create?          **3.** _____

**4.** From which tables or other queries will these new queries obtain the information? What criteria will be required to limit the total number of records produced?

| **Query Name** | **Connected Tables (or Other Queries)** |
|---|---|
| _____ | _____ |
| | _____ |
| | _____ |
| _____ | _____ |
| | _____ |
| | _____ |
| _____ | _____ |
| | _____ |
| | _____ |

| **Query Name** | **Connected Tables (or Other Queries)** |
| --- | --- |
| _____ | _____ |
| | _____ |
| | _____ |
| | _____ |
| _____ | _____ |
| | _____ |
| | _____ |
| _____ | _____ |
| | _____ |

**5.** How many forms will you create?        5. _____

**6.** What are the names of the forms? What table or tables will they be connected to?

| **Form Name** | **Connected Tables (or Queries)** |
| --- | --- |
| _____ | _____ |
| | _____ |
| | _____ |
| | _____ |
| | _____ |
| | _____ |
| _____ | _____ |
| | _____ |
| | _____ |
| | _____ |
| _____ | _____ |
| | _____ |
| | _____ |
| | _____ |
| | _____ |

**7.** How many reports will you create?                    7. _____

**8.** What are the names of the reports and where will they obtain their information?

| <u>**Report Name**</u> | <u>**What Information Will Be Used? (State whether that information will come from queries or tables.)**</u> |
|---|---|
| _____ | _____ |
|  | _____ |
|  | _____ |
| _____ | _____ |
|  | _____ |
|  | _____ |
|  | _____ |
| _____ | _____ |
|  | _____ |
|  | _____ |
| _____ | _____ |
|  | _____ |
|  | _____ |
| _____ | _____ |
|  | _____ |

**9.** What is the key piece of information that will be used to
relate all the tables together?                    9. _____

# PROJECT FIVE

# NighTech Restaurant

## Assignment 34: Design the Tables in the NighTech Database

In this assignment, you will design and create the tables in the database to handle all aspects of employment at the NighTech Restaurant. The tables should contain information on the employees themselves, as shown in the employee information form in Assignment 33. They will also maintain a running total of hours worked and the number of paychecks earned.

Some text fields will need an Input Mask to force the data to be formatted a certain way. You can choose among several commonly used masks by clicking in the Input Mask area in the lower part of the Design view of the table. Then click on the Ellipsis button ( ) to the right of the field and choose the input mask you would like with the mask wizard.

What will be the names of the tables and fields in your database design? What type and size will you set for each field? What mask will you use to format ZipCode and PhoneNumber fields so that the information fits in the space provided?

**Table Name:** _____

| **Field Name** | **Type** | **Size** | **Mask?** |
| --- | --- | --- | --- |
| _____ | _____ | _____ | _____ |
| _____ | _____ | _____ | _____ |
| _____ | _____ | _____ | _____ |
| _____ | _____ | _____ | _____ |
| _____ | _____ | _____ | _____ |
| _____ | _____ | _____ | _____ |
| _____ | _____ | _____ | _____ |
| _____ | _____ | _____ | _____ |
| _____ | _____ | _____ | _____ |
| _____ | _____ | _____ | _____ |

**Table Name:** _____

| **Field Name** | **Type** | **Size** | **Mask?** |
|----------------|----------|----------|-----------|
| _____ | _____ | _____ | _____ |
| _____ | _____ | _____ | _____ |
| _____ | _____ | _____ | _____ |
| _____ | _____ | _____ | _____ |
| _____ | _____ | _____ | _____ |
| _____ | _____ | _____ | _____ |
| _____ | _____ | _____ | _____ |
| _____ | _____ | _____ | _____ |
| _____ | _____ | _____ | _____ |

**Table Name:** _____

| **Field Name** | **Type** | **Size** | **Mask?** |
|----------------|----------|----------|-----------|
| _____ | _____ | _____ | _____ |
| _____ | _____ | _____ | _____ |
| _____ | _____ | _____ | _____ |
| _____ | _____ | _____ | _____ |
| _____ | _____ | _____ | _____ |
| _____ | _____ | _____ | _____ |
| _____ | _____ | _____ | _____ |
| _____ | _____ | _____ | _____ |
| _____ | _____ | _____ | _____ |
| _____ | _____ | _____ | _____ |
| _____ | _____ | _____ | _____ |

**Table Name:** _____

| **Field Name** | **Type** | **Size** | **Mask?** |
|---|---|---|---|
| _____ | _____ | _____ | _____ |
| _____ | _____ | _____ | _____ |
| _____ | _____ | _____ | _____ |
| _____ | _____ | _____ | _____ |
| _____ | _____ | _____ | _____ |
| _____ | _____ | _____ | _____ |
| _____ | _____ | _____ | _____ |
| _____ | _____ | _____ | _____ |
| _____ | _____ | _____ | _____ |

**Table Name:** _____

| **Field Name** | **Type** | **Size** | **Mask?** |
|---|---|---|---|
| _____ | _____ | _____ | _____ |
| _____ | _____ | _____ | _____ |
| _____ | _____ | _____ | _____ |
| _____ | _____ | _____ | _____ |
| _____ | _____ | _____ | _____ |
| _____ | _____ | _____ | _____ |
| _____ | _____ | _____ | _____ |
| _____ | _____ | _____ | _____ |
| _____ | _____ | _____ | _____ |

## PROJECT FIVE

# NighTech Restaurant

## Assignment 35: Design the Relationships and Queries in the NighTech Database

In this assignment, you will set up the relationships between the tables you created in Assignment 34. You will also design any queries you will be using.

1. Draw the tables, the related fields, and the relationship connection. Indicate which table is the 1 and which is the Many ($\infty$) side of the relationship. (You may print the relationship window from Microsoft Access and attach it if you like.

Show relationships here

**2.** Queries are used to combine information from multiple tables or to reduce the amount of information available based on certain criteria. The results of the query can then be used in a form or report, like information from a table. Decide in what forms and reports the queries will be helpful and list them here.

| Query Name | Report or Form in Which Results Will Be Used | Describe What the Query Will Do |
| --- | --- | --- |
| _____ | _____ | _____ |
|  |  | _____ |
|  |  | _____ |
| _____ | _____ | _____ |
|  |  | _____ |
|  |  | _____ |
| _____ | _____ | _____ |
|  |  | _____ |
|  |  | _____ |
|  |  | _____ |
| _____ | _____ | _____ |

**3.** Build each query and test the results. Show the design for your queries below.

**Query Name:** _____

| Field Name | From Table (or Query) | Sort? | Show? | Criteria |
|---|---|---|---|---|
| _____ | _____ | _____ | _____ | _____ |
| _____ | _____ | _____ | _____ | _____ |
| _____ | _____ | _____ | _____ | _____ |
| _____ | _____ | _____ | _____ | _____ |
| _____ | _____ | _____ | _____ | _____ |
| _____ | _____ | _____ | _____ | _____ |
| _____ | _____ | _____ | _____ | _____ |
| _____ | _____ | _____ | _____ | _____ |
| _____ | _____ | _____ | _____ | _____ |

**Query Name:** _____

| Field Name | From Table (or Query) | Sort? | Show? | Criteria |
|---|---|---|---|---|
| _____ | _____ | _____ | _____ | _____ |
| _____ | _____ | _____ | _____ | _____ |
| _____ | _____ | _____ | _____ | _____ |
| _____ | _____ | _____ | _____ | _____ |
| _____ | _____ | _____ | _____ | _____ |
| _____ | _____ | _____ | _____ | _____ |
| _____ | _____ | _____ | _____ | _____ |
| _____ | _____ | _____ | _____ | _____ |

**Query Name:** _____

| Field Name | From Table (or Query) | Sort? | Show? | Criteria |
|------------|------------------------|-------|-------|----------|
| _____ | _____ | _____ | _____ | _____ |
| _____ | _____ | _____ | _____ | _____ |
| _____ | _____ | _____ | _____ | _____ |
| _____ | _____ | _____ | _____ | _____ |
| _____ | _____ | _____ | _____ | _____ |
| _____ | _____ | _____ | _____ | _____ |
| _____ | _____ | _____ | _____ | _____ |
| _____ | _____ | _____ | _____ | _____ |
| _____ | _____ | _____ | _____ | _____ |

**Query Name:** _____

| Field Name | From Table (or Query) | Sort? | Show? | Criteria |
|------------|------------------------|-------|-------|----------|
| _____ | _____ | _____ | _____ | _____ |
| _____ | _____ | _____ | _____ | _____ |
| _____ | _____ | _____ | _____ | _____ |
| _____ | _____ | _____ | _____ | _____ |
| _____ | _____ | _____ | _____ | _____ |
| _____ | _____ | _____ | _____ | _____ |
| _____ | _____ | _____ | _____ | _____ |
| _____ | _____ | _____ | _____ | _____ |
| _____ | _____ | _____ | _____ | _____ |

A special query called a summation query allows you to perform a query whose results are grouped by one or more fields. A group is created for each unique value of a field. For example, if you have a field called JobTitle for each employee, you can create a summation query that results in the creation of one record that totals the pay of all the Cooks and one record that totals the pay for all the Cashiers. You can create a summation query by following the steps listed below.

- Create a new query.
- Select fields and expressions for each of the fields in the query result.
- Right-click over the bottom half of the Query window (over the line for Field) and select the Totals ( Σ Totals ) option. A new line called *Total:* will appear. From the Total: field, you can select several options including the following:

**Group by:** Groups records with the same value for the given field into the same result.

**Sum:** Calculates the sum of the values of the field within each group. This option works only with numerical fields.

**Count:** Shows the number of records in a group.

**Expression:** Displays the result of an expression (see the next paragraph.)

Another useful feature of the query builder is the capability of using expressions in place of fields from tables in the field area. Many different types of equations can be used. Used this way, a query acts something like a ledger (or a spreadsheet program) by performing equations on each record available to the query. The figure below shows the design of a summation query to calculate the time worked each day.

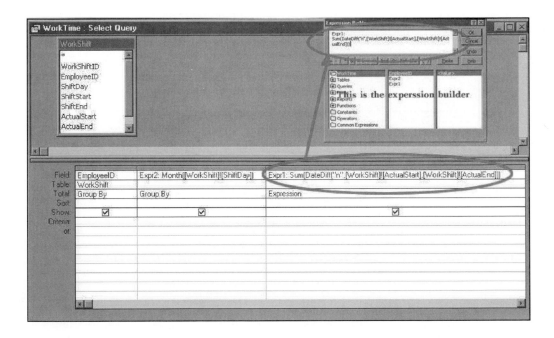

Two important equations, which you may need, are shown. They can be added by right-clicking over the field row for the column in which you want to build an equation and choosing the *Build* ( ◣ Build... )button. In the large area at the top, type in the equation.

To calculate the month of a date so you can group work time by month, the equation is:

$$\texttt{=Month([WorkShift]![ShiftDay])}$$

The equation returns the month as a number from 1 to 12 for the ShiftDay field in the WorkShift table.

To calculate the time worked, use an equation called *DateDiff*. DateDiff returns a single number that represents the number of minutes, hours, days, etc. Type in the expressions below, but replace the table and field names (which appear inside the brackets) with *your* table names and field names.

`=Sum(DateDiff("n",[WorkShift]![ActualStart],[WorkShift]! [ActualEnd]))`

The equation returns the summation of the differences between the time in the field, ActualEnd and ActualStart, both from the WorkShift table. The *n* in the equation means that the value returned is in minutes. If you want the value in hours, you can use an *h* in place of the *n*. You should be aware, however, that the number returned is an integer, so *h* cannot return 3.5 hours: it would return the number 4.

**4.** Create any summation queries that you need and enter the information below.

**Summation Query Name:** _____

| No. | Field Name or Expression | From Table (or Query) |
|-----|--------------------------|-----------------------|
| 1 | _____ | _____ |
| 2 | _____ | _____ |
| 3 | _____ | _____ |
| 4 | _____ | _____ |

| No. | How Totaled? | Sorted? | Criteria |
|-----|--------------|---------|----------|
| 1 | _____ | _____ | _____ |
| 2 | _____ | _____ | _____ |
| 3 | _____ | _____ | _____ |
| 4 | _____ | _____ | _____ |

**Summation Query Name:** _____

| No. | Field Name or Expression | From Table (or Query) |
|---|---|---|
| 1 | _____ | _____ |
| 2 | _____ | _____ |
| 3 | _____ | _____ |
| 4 | _____ | _____ |

| No. | How Totaled? | Sorted? | Criteria |
|---|---|---|---|
| 1 | _____ | _____ | _____ |
| 2 | _____ | _____ | _____ |
| 3 | _____ | _____ | _____ |
| 4 | _____ | _____ | _____ |

PROJECT FIVE    NighTech Restaurant

## Assignment 36: Design Employee Information Form and Enter Employee Information

Using the form shown in Assignment 33 and the table you created in Assignment 34, you will need to design a form to view and enter basic employee information. Once this form has been created, you will need to enter the information for employees hired before the restaurant officially opens.

1. Show the design of your form in the space provided. You may print a copy of the form from Microsoft Access, if you like. In the space allotted for entry, write the name of the field that contains the information displayed.

Show form design here.

2. Using the form you designed, enter employee information for the following 24 new employees.

LAST NAME:  Abbott          FIRST NAME:  Jane                    MI:  T
SSN:  309-22-8351           DATE OF BIRTH:  11/30/1981          Married?
STREET ADDRESS:  1801 Windmill Lane
CITY:  Herndon              PHONE NO:  (703) 555-8266
STATE:  VA ZIP CODE:  22835-0002      CELL PHONE NO:  (703) 555-9011
PAY RATE:  $6.50            START DATE:  1/2/2002          RELEASE DATE:
JOB TITLE:  Cashier         FULL TIME/PART TIME:  Part Time


LAST NAME:  Barazia         FIRST NAME:  Elvira                  MI:
SSN:  317-40-0989           DATE OF BIRTH:  9/15/1958          Married?
STREET ADDRESS:  1310 Foxridge Apts.
CITY:  Reston               PHONE NO:  (703) 555-2099
STATE:  VA ZIP CODE:  22455-4030      CELL PHONE NO:  (703) 555-9033
PAY RATE:  $15.00           START DATE:  1/2/2002          RELEASE DATE:
JOB TITLE:  Manager         FULL TIME/PART TIME:  Full Time


LAST NAME:  Dumez           FIRST NAME:  Alexander              MI:  W
SSN:  384-20-9226           DATE OF BIRTH:  3/26/1965          Married?
STREET ADDRESS:  2736 Calloway Street
CITY:  Chantilly            PHONE NO:  (703) 555-3404
STATE:  VA ZIP CODE:  22855-2001      CELL PHONE NO:  (703) 555-9309
PAY RATE:  $6.50            START DATE:  1/7/2002          RELEASE DATE:
JOB TITLE:  Cook            FULL TIME/PART TIME:  Part Time


LAST NAME:  Fiorello        FIRST NAME:  Jacque                 MI:  R
SSN:  342-90-6321           DATE OF BIRTH:  6/13/1979          Married?
STREET ADDRESS:  3405 Albemaro St. NW
CITY:  Washington           PHONE NO:  (202) 555-2355
STATE:  DC ZIP CODE:  20034-3452      CELL PHONE NO:  (703) 555-9503
PAY RATE:  $7.00            START DATE:  1/7/2002          RELEASE DATE:
JOB TITLE:  Host            FULL TIME/PART TIME:  Part Time


LAST NAME:  Gomez-Salley  FIRST NAME:  Oscar                    MI:  T
SSN:  281-44-6082           DATE OF BIRTH:  5/8/1970           Married?
STREET ADDRESS:  503 Chain Bridge Rd. #304
CITY:  Fairfax              PHONE NO:  (703) 555-8338
STATE:  VA ZIP CODE:  22105-3553      CELL PHONE NO:  (703) 555-9350
PAY RATE:  $9.50            START DATE:  1/14/200         RELEASE DATE:
JOB TITLE:  Wine Steward  FULL TIME/PART TIME:  Full Time

LAST NAME: Johnson        FIRST NAME: Monica            MI: A
SSN: 375-15-3465          DATE OF BIRTH: 10/19/1973     Married?
STREET ADDRESS: H-1 Apartment Heights
CITY: Reston              PHONE NO: (703) 555-8590
STATE: VA ZIP CODE: 22355-         CELL PHONE NO: (703) 555-9341
PAY RATE: $6.75           START DATE: 1/14/200          RELEASE DATE:
JOB TITLE: Server         FULL TIME/PART TIME: Part Time


LAST NAME: Kasturi       FIRST NAME: Prahla            MI:
SSN: 347-28-6385          DATE OF BIRTH: 2/22/1977      Married?
STREET ADDRESS: 10344 Wilson Blvd Apt 1234
CITY: Arlington          PHONE NO: (703) 555-4599
STATE: VA ZIP CODE: 21334-         CELL PHONE NO: (703) 555-9405
PAY RATE: $6.50           START DATE: 1/21/200          RELEASE DATE:
JOB TITLE: Cook          FULL TIME/PART TIME: Part Time


LAST NAME: LaCorte       FIRST NAME: Gerald            MI: D
SSN: 421-38-2347          DATE OF BIRTH: 8/17/1974      Married?
STREET ADDRESS: 3055 S. Main Street
CITY: Berryville         PHONE NO: (540) 555-3533
STATE: VA ZIP CODE: 23221-0350     CELL PHONE NO: (540) 555-9350
PAY RATE: $10.00          START DATE: 1/7/2002          RELEASE DATE:
JOB TITLE: Asst. Manager FULL TIME/PART TIME: Full Time


LAST NAME: London        FIRST NAME: Maria             MI: R
SSN: 306-74-6397          DATE OF BIRTH: 7/14/1971      Married?
STREET ADDRESS: 3439 Anthem Way
CITY: Arlington          PHONE NO: (703) 555-3145
STATE: VA ZIP CODE: 21344-         CELL PHONE NO: (703) 555-9303
PAY RATE: $6.75           START DATE: 1/14/200          RELEASE DATE:
JOB TITLE: Server         FULL TIME/PART TIME: Full Time


LAST NAME: Maas          FIRST NAME: Alexis            MI: G
SSN: 385-64-3386          DATE OF BIRTH: 11/1/1968      Married?
STREET ADDRESS: 5545 Amherst Dr.
CITY: Springfield        PHONE NO: (703) 555-9344
STATE: VA ZIP CODE: 22151-         CELL PHONE NO:
PAY RATE: $6.50           START DATE: 1/21/200          RELEASE DATE:
JOB TITLE: Cook          FULL TIME/PART TIME: Part Time

LAST NAME: McGarry          FIRST NAME: Scott              MI: J
SSN: 411-62-8120           DATE OF BIRTH: 5/20/1959        Married?
STREET ADDRESS: 2304 Braddock Rd. Apt 3002
CITY: Annandale            PHONE NO: (703) 555-2331
STATE: VA ZIP CODE: 21995-           CELL PHONE NO: (703) 555-9502
PAY RATE: $7.20            START DATE: 1/21/200           RELEASE DATE:
JOB TITLE: Custodian       FULL TIME/PART TIME: Full Time


LAST NAME: Morrison        FIRST NAME: Helena             MI: J
SSN: 236-41-1265           DATE OF BIRTH: 6/21/1962        Married?
STREET ADDRESS: 1613 Palmento Circle
CITY: Great Falls          PHONE NO: (703) 555-1103
STATE: VA ZIP CODE: 21035-           CELL PHONE NO: (703) 555-9315
PAY RATE: $10.55           START DATE: 1/7/2002           RELEASE DATE:
JOB TITLE: Asst. Manager FULL TIME/PART TIME: Full Time


LAST NAME: Ngan            FIRST NAME: Yi-Pheng            MI:
SSN: 293-62-6113           DATE OF BIRTH: 2/18/1982        Married?
STREET ADDRESS: 824 Whispering Pine Dr
CITY: Burke                PHONE NO: (703) 555-0239
STATE: VA ZIP CODE: 22345-           CELL PHONE NO: (703) 555-9133
PAY RATE: $6.75            START DATE: 1/21/200           RELEASE DATE:
JOB TITLE: Server          FULL TIME/PART TIME: Part Time


LAST NAME: Niehaus         FIRST NAME: Susan              MI: K
SSN: 361-26-0916           DATE OF BIRTH: 4/18/1973        Married?
STREET ADDRESS: 10614 Dunkirk Ct
CITY: Chantilly            PHONE NO: (703) 555-3398
STATE: VA ZIP CODE: 22698-           CELL PHONE NO: (703) 555-9591
PAY RATE: $10.50           START DATE: 1/7/2002           RELEASE DATE:
JOB TITLE: Asst. Manager FULL TIME/PART TIME: Full Time


LAST NAME: O'Rourke        FIRST NAME: Allison             MI: Y
SSN: 350-38-4332           DATE OF BIRTH: 5/9/1981         Married?
STREET ADDRESS: 12345 Duke St. #443
CITY: Alexandria           PHONE NO: (703) 555-8122
STATE: VA ZIP CODE: 22103-           CELL PHONE NO: (703) 993-2344
PAY RATE: $6.75            START DATE: 1/7/2002           RELEASE DATE:
JOB TITLE: Server          FULL TIME/PART TIME: Part Time

LAST NAME: Pace          FIRST NAME: William          MI: D
SSN: 332-85-9163         DATE OF BIRTH: 9/5/1979       Married?
STREET ADDRESS: 1820 Park Manor Dr.
CITY: Herndon            PHONE NO: (703) 555-6604
STATE: VA ZIP CODE: 23553-          CELL PHONE NO:
PAY RATE: $6.50          START DATE: 1/28/200          RELEASE DATE:
JOB TITLE: Cashier       FULL TIME/PART TIME: Part Time


LAST NAME: Peoples       FIRST NAME: Louisa           MI: S
SSN: 356-72-1549         DATE OF BIRTH: 3/16/1977      Married?
STREET ADDRESS: 6344 Telegraph Rd. #1245
CITY: Alexandria         PHONE NO: (703) 555-4014
STATE: VA ZIP CODE: 21693-          CELL PHONE NO: (703) 555-9698
PAY RATE: $6.75          START DATE: 1/28/200          RELEASE DATE:
JOB TITLE: Server        FULL TIME/PART TIME: Part Time


LAST NAME: Rezvani       FIRST NAME: Mohamed          MI: A
SSN: 349-17-7258         DATE OF BIRTH: 12/24/1969     Married?
STREET ADDRESS: 33 East Market St.
CITY: Reston             PHONE NO: (703) 555-4039
STATE: VA ZIP CODE: 22450-          CELL PHONE NO: (703) 555-9348
PAY RATE: $6.00          START DATE: 2/4/2002          RELEASE DATE:
JOB TITLE: Cook          FULL TIME/PART TIME: Part Time


LAST NAME: Rodriguez     FIRST NAME: David            MI: R
SSN: 378-62-6514         DATE OF BIRTH: 2/20/1978      Married?
STREET ADDRESS: 9330 Ashton Ave.
CITY: Manassas           PHONE NO: (703) 555-2967
STATE: VA ZIP CODE: 22110-          CELL PHONE NO:
PAY RATE: $6.75          START DATE: 2/4/2002          RELEASE DATE:
JOB TITLE: Server        FULL TIME/PART TIME: Part Time


LAST NAME: Savino        FIRST NAME: Durado           MI: L
SSN: 371-62-3519         DATE OF BIRTH: 8/27/1964      Married?
STREET ADDRESS: 827 Potomac Ave.
CITY: Great Falls        PHONE NO: (703) 555-3878
STATE: VA ZIP CODE: 22034-          CELL PHONE NO: (703) 555-9094
PAY RATE: $15.50         START DATE: 1/7/2002          RELEASE DATE:
JOB TITLE: Accountant    FULL TIME/PART TIME: Full Time

LAST NAME:  Schulz          FIRST NAME:  Ann                          MI:  G
SSN:  410-71-7295           DATE OF BIRTH:  10/18/1981        Married?
STREET ADDRESS:  2034 9th St SE
CITY:  Washington           PHONE NO:  (202) 555-3444
STATE:  DC ZIP CODE:  20034-           CELL PHONE NO:  (202) 555-9345
PAY RATE:  $6.50            START DATE:  2/4/2002        RELEASE DATE:
JOB TITLE:  Server          FULL TIME/PART TIME:  Part Time

LAST NAME:  Shean          FIRST NAME:  Colleen                      MI:
SSN:  385-25-0140           DATE OF BIRTH:  7/22/1976        Married?
STREET ADDRESS:  2711 Chelsea Square, #1534
CITY:  Rossalyn            PHONE NO:  (703) 555-3461
STATE:  VA ZIP CODE:  20943-           CELL PHONE NO:  (703) 555-8994
PAY RATE:  $10.25           START DATE:  2/4/2002        RELEASE DATE:
JOB TITLE:  Receiving Manager          FULL TIME/PART TIME:  Full Time

LAST NAME:  Van Dyke          FIRST NAME:  Kenneth                   MI:  W
SSN:  246-88-9351           DATE OF BIRTH:  9/18/1977        Married?
STREET ADDRESS:  15394 Braddock Rd. #4340
CITY:  Centerville          PHONE NO:  (703) 555-4138
STATE:  VA ZIP CODE:  22234-           CELL PHONE NO:  (703) 555-8923
PAY RATE:  $6.75            START DATE:  2/11/200        RELEASE DATE:
JOB TITLE:  Server          FULL TIME/PART TIME:  Part Time

LAST NAME:  Wong          FIRST NAME:  Matthew                       MI:
SSN:  396-36-8265           DATE OF BIRTH:  6/28/1980        Married?
STREET ADDRESS:  2540 Stonegate Drive #443
CITY:  Manassas            PHONE NO:  (703) 555-3411
STATE:  VA ZIP CODE:  22110-           CELL PHONE NO:  (703) 555-8322
PAY RATE:  $6.00            START DATE:  2/11/200        RELEASE DATE:
JOB TITLE:  Cook           FULL TIME/PART TIME:  Part Time

## PROJECT FIVE NighTech Restaurant

## Assignment 37: Design Employee Time Schedule and Enter Schedule Information

Use the form labeled Employee Work Schedule shown in Assignment 33 and the table you created in Assignment 34 that contains information about work times for each employee to design a form showing the schedule for a particular employee. You do not need to worry about how to search for a particular employee. You will use the navigation buttons to find each one.

1. Show the design of your form here. You may print a copy of the form from Microsoft Access if you like.

Show form design here.

**2.** Enter the following schedule information. Replace the dates with those of the current week.

---

NAME      Morrison     Helena             SSN    236-41-1265
          LAST        FIRST

JOB TITLE   Asst. Manager

| Date | Scheduled Start | Scheduled End |
|------|-----------------|---------------|
| Tuesday, January 08, 2002 | 3:00:00 PM | 11:00:00 PM |
| Wednesday, January 09, 2002 | 3:00:00 PM | 11:00:00 PM |
| Thursday, January 10, 2002 | 3:00:00 PM | 11:00:00 PM |
| Friday, January 11, 2002 | 3:00:00 PM | 11:00:00 PM |
| Saturday, January 12, 2002 | 3:00:00 PM | 11:45:00 PM |

---

NAME      Van Dyke     Kenneth            SSN    246-88-9351
          LAST        FIRST

JOB TITLE   Server

| Date | Scheduled Start | Scheduled End |
|------|-----------------|---------------|
| Tuesday, January 08, 2002 | 4:30:00 PM | 9:30:00 PM |
| Wednesday, January 09, 2002 | 4:30:00 PM | 9:30:00 PM |
| Thursday, January 10, 2002 | 4:30:00 PM | 9:30:00 PM |
| Friday, January 11, 2002 | 4:30:00 PM | 9:30:00 PM |
| Saturday, January 12, 2002 | 5:30:00 PM | 11:00:00 PM |

---

NAME      Gomez-Salley Oscar           SSN    281-44-6082
          LAST        FIRST

JOB TITLE   Wine Steward

| Date | Scheduled Start | Scheduled End |
|------|-----------------|---------------|
| Tuesday, January 08, 2002 | 3:00:00 PM | 9:00:00 PM |
| Wednesday, January 09, 2002 | 3:00:00 PM | 9:00:00 PM |
| Thursday, January 10, 2002 | 5:00:00 PM | 11:30:00 PM |
| Friday, January 11, 2002 | 5:00:00 PM | 11:30:00 PM |
| Saturday, January 12, 2002 | 5:00:00 PM | 11:30:00 PM |
| Monday, January 14, 2002 | 12:00:00 PM | 6:30:00 PM |

---

NAME      Ngan        Yi-Pheng          SSN    293-62-6113
          LAST        FIRST

JOB TITLE   Server

| Date | Scheduled Start | Scheduled End |
|------|-----------------|---------------|
| Friday, January 11, 2002 | 5:00:00 PM | 11:00:00 PM |
| Saturday, January 12, 2002 | 5:00:00 PM | 11:00:00 PM |

| NAME | Abbott | Jane | | SSN | 309-22-8351 |
| | LAST | FIRST | | | |

JOB TITLE  Cashier

| **Date** | **Scheduled Start** | **Scheduled End** |
| --- | --- | --- |
| Tuesday, January 08, 2002 | 4:00:00 PM | 9:00:00 PM |
| Wednesday, January 09, 2002 | 4:00:00 PM | 9:00:00 PM |
| Thursday, January 10, 2002 | 4:00:00 PM | 10:30:00 PM |
| Friday, January 11, 2002 | 4:00:00 PM | 10:30:00 PM |
| Saturday, January 12, 2002 | 5:00:00 PM | 11:30:00 PM |

| NAME | Barazia | Elvira | | SSN | 317-40-0989 |
| | LAST | FIRST | | | |

JOB TITLE  Manager

| **Date** | **Scheduled Start** | **Scheduled End** |
| --- | --- | --- |
| Monday, January 07, 2002 | 10:00:00 AM | 6:00:00 PM |
| Tuesday, January 08, 2002 | 10:00:00 AM | 6:00:00 PM |
| Wednesday, January 09, 2002 | 10:00:00 AM | 6:00:00 PM |
| Thursday, January 10, 2002 | 10:00:00 AM | 6:00:00 PM |
| Friday, January 11, 2002 | 11:00:00 AM | 9:00:00 PM |
| Saturday, January 12, 2002 | 12:00:00 PM | 11:00:00 PM |

| NAME | Pace | William | | SSN | 332-85-9163 |
| | LAST | FIRST | | | |

JOB TITLE  Cashier

| **Date** | **Scheduled Start** | **Scheduled End** |
| --- | --- | --- |
| Monday, January 07, 2002 | 10:00:00 AM | 4:30:00 PM |
| Tuesday, January 08, 2002 | 10:00:00 AM | 4:30:00 PM |
| Wednesday, January 09, 2002 | 10:00:00 AM | 4:30:00 PM |
| Thursday, January 10, 2002 | 10:00:00 AM | 4:30:00 PM |
| Friday, January 11, 2002 | 10:00:00 AM | 7:30:00 PM |
| Saturday, January 12, 2002 | 10:00:00 AM | 7:30:00 PM |

| NAME | Fiorello | Jacque | | SSN | 342-90-6321 |
| | LAST | FIRST | | | |

JOB TITLE  Host

| **Date** | **Scheduled Start** | **Scheduled End** |
| --- | --- | --- |
| Monday, January 07, 2002 | 5:00:00 PM | 11:30:00 PM |
| Tuesday, January 08, 2002 | 5:00:00 PM | 11:30:00 PM |
| Wednesday, January 09, 2002 | 5:00:00 PM | 11:30:00 PM |
| Thursday, January 10, 2002 | 5:00:00 PM | 11:30:00 PM |
| Friday, January 11, 2002 | 5:00:00 PM | 11:30:00 PM |
| Saturday, January 12, 2002 | 4:00:00 PM | 11:30:00 PM |

NAME       Kasturi     Prahla               SSN    347-28-6385
             LAST       FIRST

JOB TITLE  Cook

| Date | Scheduled Start | Scheduled End |
| --- | --- | --- |
| Monday, January 07, 2002 | 4:00:00 PM | 11:00:00 PM |
| Tuesday, January 08, 2002 | 4:00:00 PM | 11:00:00 PM |
| Wednesday, January 09, 2002 | 4:00:00 PM | 11:00:00 PM |
| Thursday, January 10, 2002 | 4:00:00 PM | 11:00:00 PM |
| Friday, January 11, 2002 | 4:00:00 PM | 11:45:00 PM |
| Saturday, January 12, 2002 | 4:00:00 PM | 11:45:00 PM |

NAME       Rezvani     Mohamed          SSN    349-17-7258
             LAST       FIRST

JOB TITLE  Cook

| Date | Scheduled Start | Scheduled End |
| --- | --- | --- |
| Monday, January 07, 2002 | 5:00:00 PM | 11:00:00 PM |
| Tuesday, January 08, 2002 | 5:00:00 PM | 11:00:00 PM |
| Wednesday, January 09, 2002 | 5:00:00 PM | 11:00:00 PM |
| Thursday, January 10, 2002 | 5:00:00 PM | 11:00:00 PM |
| Friday, January 11, 2002 | 4:00:00 PM | 11:30:00 PM |
| Saturday, January 12, 2002 | 4:00:00 PM | 11:30:00 PM |

NAME       Niehaus     Susan            SSN    361-26-0916
             LAST       FIRST

JOB TITLE  Asst. Manager

| Date | Scheduled Start | Scheduled End |
| --- | --- | --- |
| Monday, January 07, 2002 | 4:30:00 PM | 11:00:00 PM |
| Tuesday, January 08, 2002 | 4:30:00 PM | 11:00:00 PM |
| Wednesday, January 09, 2002 | 4:30:00 PM | 11:00:00 PM |
| Thursday, January 10, 2002 | 4:30:00 PM | 11:00:00 PM |
| Friday, January 11, 2002 | 4:00:00 PM | 11:45:00 PM |
| Saturday, January 12, 2002 | 4:00:00 PM | 11:45:00 PM |

NAME       Wong      Matthew          SSN    396-36-8265
             LAST       FIRST

JOB TITLE  Cook

| Date | Scheduled Start | Scheduled End |
| --- | --- | --- |
| Monday, January 07, 2002 | 12:00:00 PM | 6:00:00 PM |
| Tuesday, January 08, 2002 | 12:00:00 PM | 6:00:00 PM |
| Wednesday, January 09, 2002 | 12:00:00 PM | 6:00:00 PM |
| Thursday, January 10, 2002 | 12:00:00 PM | 7:00:00 PM |
| Friday, January 11, 2002 | 12:00:00 PM | 8:00:00 PM |
| Saturday, January 12, 2002 | 12:00:00 PM | 8:00:00 PM |

## PROJECT FIVE

# NighTech Restaurant

## Assignment 38: Design Manager's Time-Clock Form and Enter Actual Times Worked

Based on the requirements stated in Assignment 33 and the table you created in Assignment 34 that contains information about actual times each employee worked, design a form showing the schedule for work on a particular day. You will also need to create a query that gathers the correct information and uses a criteria to limit the items shown to a particular date. *Note: This may be a modification of a query you created in Assignment 35.*

1. Instead of putting an actual date in the query (such as *#1/12/2000#*), you can ask for the date by setting your criteria to *[Enter the Date:]*. Access looks for a variable or field name called *EntertheDate.* When it does not find it, a small window appears on the screen with a message and an area in which to put the value. Show your query information in the table below.

**Query Name:** _____

| Field Name | From Table (or Query) | Sort? | Show? | Criteria |
|---|---|---|---|---|
| _____ | _____ | _____ | _____ | _____ |
| _____ | _____ | _____ | _____ | _____ |
| _____ | _____ | _____ | _____ | _____ |
| _____ | _____ | _____ | _____ | _____ |
| _____ | _____ | _____ | _____ | _____ |
| _____ | _____ | _____ | _____ | _____ |
| _____ | _____ | _____ | _____ | _____ |
| _____ | _____ | _____ | _____ | _____ |
| _____ | _____ | _____ | _____ | _____ |

**2.** Show the design of your form here. You may print a copy of the form from Microsoft Access if you like.

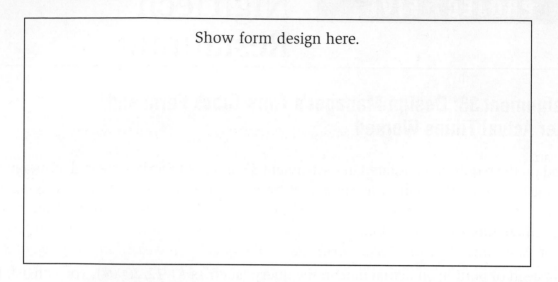

Show form design here.

**3.** Enter the following Clock-In and Clock-Out times. Note that the dates should be for the week that you performed Assignment 37.

**Note:** Change the dates to match the worktime dates you entered in Assignment 37.

**Date:** **Monday, January 07, 2002**

| Last Name | First Name | SSN | Job Title | Clock In | Clock Out |
|-----------|------------|-----|-----------|----------|-----------|
| Barazia | Elvira | 317-40-0989 | Manager | 9:30:00 AM | 6:12:00 PM |
| Fiorello | Jacque | 342-90-6321 | Host | 4:55:00 PM | 11:45:00 PM |
| Kasturi | Prahla | 347-28-6385 | Cook | 4:02:00 PM | 11:05:00 PM |
| Niehaus | Susan | 361-26-0916 | Asst. Manager | 4:47:00 PM | 11:00:00 PM |
| Pace | William | 332-85-9163 | Cashier | 10:02:00 AM | 4:35:00 PM |
| Rezvani | Mohamed | 349-17-7258 | Cook | 4:49:00 PM | 11:10:00 PM |
| Wong | Matthew | 396-36-8265 | Cook | 12:01:00 PM | 6:05:00 PM |

**Date:** <u>Tuesday, January 08, 2002</u>

| Last Name | First Name | SSN | Job Title | Clock In | Clock Out |
|---|---|---|---|---|---|
| Abbott | Jane | 309-22-8351 | Cashier | 3:55:00 PM | 9:01:00 PM |
| Barazia | Elvira | 317-40-0989 | Manager | 10:02:00 AM | 6:00:00 PM |
| Fiorello | Jacque | 342-90-6321 | Host | 4:59:00 PM | 11:32:00 PM |
| Gomez-Salley | Oscar | 281-44-6082 | Wine Steward | 3:01:00 PM | 8:58:00 PM |
| Kasturi | Prahla | 347-28-6385 | Cook | 4:05:00 PM | 11:01:00 PM |
| Morrison | Helena | 236-41-1265 | Asst. Manager | 3:01:00 PM | 11:08:00 PM |
| Niehaus | Susan | 361-26-0916 | Asst. Manager | 4:30:00 PM | 10:52:00 PM |
| Pace | William | 332-85-9163 | Cashier | 9:52:00 AM | 4:32:00 PM |
| Rezvani | Mohamed | 349-17-7258 | Cook | 5:02:00 PM | 11:00:00 PM |
| Van Dyke | Kenneth | 246-88-9351 | Server | 4:41:00 PM | 9:32:00 PM |
| Wong | Matthew | 396-36-8265 | Cook | 11:50:00 AM | 6:12:00 PM |

**Date:** <u>Wednesday, January 09, 2002</u>

| Last Name | First Name | SSN | Job Title | Clock In | Clock Out |
|---|---|---|---|---|---|
| Abbott | Jane | 309-22-8351 | Cashier | 4:01:00 PM | 8:55:00 PM |
| Barazia | Elvira | 317-40-0989 | Manager | 9:43:00 AM | 6:23:00 PM |
| Fiorello | Jacque | 342-90-6321 | Host | 4:55:00 PM | 11:28:00 PM |
| Gomez-Salley | Oscar | 281-44-6082 | Wine Steward | 2:55:00 PM | 9:01:00 PM |
| Kasturi | Prahla | 347-28-6385 | Cook | 4:00:00 PM | 11:01:00 PM |
| Morrison | Helena | 236-41-1265 | Asst. Manager | 3:10:00 PM | 11:05:00 PM |
| Niehaus | Susan | 361-26-0916 | Asst. Manager | 4:23:00 PM | 10:58:00 PM |
| Pace | William | 332-85-9163 | Cashier | 9:53:00 AM | 4:47:00 PM |
| Rezvani | Mohamed | 349-17-7258 | Cook | 5:00:00 PM | 11:00:00 PM |
| Van Dyke | Kenneth | 246-88-9351 | Server | 4:27:00 PM | 9:23:00 PM |
| Wong | Matthew | 396-36-8265 | Cook | 11:52:00 AM | 6:05:00 PM |

**Date:** <u>Thursday, January 10, 2002</u>

| Last Name | First Name | SSN | Job Title | Clock In | Clock Out |
|---|---|---|---|---|---|
| Abbott | Jane | 309-22-8351 | Cashier | 4:03:00 PM | 10:23:00 PM |
| Barazia | Elvira | 317-40-0989 | Manager | 10:00:00 AM | 6:01:00 PM |
| Fiorello | Jacque | 342-90-6321 | Host | 4:58:00 PM | 11:33:00 PM |
| Gomez-Salley | Oscar | 281-44-6082 | Wine Steward | 4:58:00 PM | 11:37:00 PM |
| Kasturi | Prahla | 347-28-6385 | Cook | 3:41:00 PM | 11:12:00 PM |
| Morrison | Helena | 236-41-1265 | Asst. Manager | 3:29:00 PM | 11:20:00 PM |
| Niehaus | Susan | 361-26-0916 | Asst. Manager | 4:32:00 PM | 10:57:00 PM |
| Pace | William | 332-85-9163 | Cashier | 9:52:00 AM | 5:05:00 PM |
| Rezvani | Mohamed | 349-17-7258 | Cook | 4:59:00 PM | 11:03:00 PM |
| Van Dyke | Kenneth | 246-88-9351 | Server | 4:22:00 PM | 9:25:00 PM |
| Wong | Matthew | 396-36-8265 | Cook | 12:00:00 PM | 7:01:00 PM |

**Date:** Friday, January 11, 2002

| Last Name | First Name | SSN | Job Title | Clock In | Clock Out |
|---|---|---|---|---|---|
| Abbott | Jane | 309-22-8351 | Cashier | 4:00:00 PM | 10:32:00 PM |
| Barazia | Elvira | 317-40-0989 | Manager | 11:02:00 PM | 9:01:00 PM |
| Fiorello | Jacque | 342-90-6321 | Host | 5:01:00 PM | 11:50:00 PM |
| Gomez-Salley | Oscar | 281-44-6082 | Wine Steward | 5:02:00 PM | 11:53:00 PM |
| Kasturi | Prahla | 347-28-6385 | Cook | 4:04:00 PM | 11:59:00 PM |
| Morrison | Helena | 236-41-1265 | Asst. Manager | 2:55:00 PM | 11:01:00 PM |
| Ngan | Yi-Pheng | 293-62-6113 | Server | 5:00:00 PM | 11:03:00 PM |
| Niehaus | Susan | 361-26-0916 | Asst. Manager | 3:59:00 PM | 11:42:00 PM |
| Pace | William | 332-85-9163 | Cashier | 9:49:00 AM | 7:33:00 PM |
| Rezvani | Mohamed | 349-17-7258 | Cook | 4:05:00 PM | 11:29:00 PM |
| Van Dyke | Kenneth | 246-88-9351 | Server | 4:29:00 PM | 9:31:00 PM |
| Wong | Matthew | 396-36-8265 | Cook | 11:48:00 AM | 8:02:00 PM |

**Date:** Saturday, January 12, 2002

| Last Name | First Name | SSN | Job Title | Clock In | Clock Out |
|---|---|---|---|---|---|
| Abbott | Jane | 309-22-8351 | Cashier | 5:01:00 PM | 11:32:00 PM |
| Barazia | Elvira | 317-40-0989 | Manager | 11:58:00 PM | 10:52:00 PM |
| Fiorello | Jacque | 342-90-6321 | Host | 4:01:00 PM | 11:30:00 PM |
| Gomez-Salley | Oscar | 281-44-6082 | Wine Steward | 5:23:00 PM | 11:29:00 PM |
| Kasturi | Prahla | 347-28-6385 | Cook | 3:55:00 PM | 11:42:00 PM |
| Morrison | Helena | 236-41-1265 | Asst. Manager | 3:08:00 PM | 11:57:00 PM |
| Ngan | Yi-Pheng | 293-62-6113 | Server | 5:00:00 PM | 11:00:00 PM |
| Niehaus | Susan | 361-26-0916 | Asst. Manager | 4:02:00 PM | 11:38:00 PM |
| Pace | William | 332-85-9163 | Cashier | 9:50:00 AM | 7:39:00 PM |
| Rezvani | Mohamed | 349-17-7258 | Cook | 3:58:00 PM | 11:32:00 PM |
| Van Dyke | Kenneth | 246-88-9351 | Server | 5:25:00 PM | 11:02:00 PM |
| Wong | Matthew | 396-36-8265 | Cook | 12:05:00 PM | 8:00:00 PM |

**PROJECT FIVE** NighTech
Restaurant

## Assignment 39: Design Employee Work Summary Report

Based on the requirements stated in Assignment 33, the table you created in Assignment 34 that contains information about work times for each employee, and the summation query you designed in Assignment 35 that contains the total time worked for each employee, design a report that displays the time worked for each employee.

1. Create a new report by following these steps.

   - Click on the Report tab of the Database window.
   - Click on *New*.
   - Choose Report Wizard and click OK.
   - Choose the fields you want to show in the report. You should use one table and one query. The table showing information about the employee must be used. The query that calculates the time worked must also be used. Write below the fields you will use.

| Table or Query Name | Field Name |
|---|---|
| _____ | _____ |
| _____ | _____ |
| _____ | _____ |
| _____ | _____ |
| _____ | _____ |
| _____ | _____ |
| _____ | _____ |
| _____ | _____ |

|              Field Name              |              Field Name              |
| ------------------------------------ | ------------------------------------ |
| _____ | _____ |
| _____ | _____ |
| _____ | _____ |
| _____ | _____ |
| _____ | _____ |
| _____ | _____ |

- Click *Next*. You will be asked how you want to view your data. Choose the table that contains information about your employees.
- Click *Next*. There should be no need to choose a grouping. Click *Next* again.
- Choose the day worked as the primary sort criteria.
- Click on the button called *Summary Options*.
- Choose the Sum option for the expression that calculates the time worked. Make sure that Detail and Summary is checked and click *OK*.
- Click *Next*. Choose a layout and click *Next*.
- Choose a report style. Click *Next*.
- Name the report. Write the name here. _____
- Click *Finish*.

2. Modify the report. A few problems with the report will need to be addressed.

- Click on the Design 🔲 button on the toolbar to make changes to the report. You can click and drag components such as Detail and Summary within their areas. You can also change the sizes of various components by dragging from the black size handles at the edges of each item. These size handles appear when you click on the item, thus selecting it for modification.
- To change the text in a label, click on the label to select it. Then click on the text to change to Insert mode. This option allows you to delete, backspace, and type new characters.
- Labels and the values associated with each are connected. They can be dragged together. The process of modifying the report is similar to modifying a form.
- You will want to add a field in the report to calculate the pay. The instructor will guide you through this process.

3. Print the final report and submit it to your instructor.

| PROJECT FIVE | NighTech Restaurant |
|---|---|

## Assignment 40: Project Quiz

Before you take this quiz, you should have completed the previous assignments so that the NighTech employee database is updated. You will use the employee database to answer the questions. You may have to create filters or queries to answer some questions.

1. What is the hourly wage of the employee whose social security number is 347-28-6385?

1. _____

2. In what month is Monica A. Johnson's birthday?

2. _____

3. What type is the Wage field of the Employee table?

3. _____

4. How many employees hold the position of Cook?

4. _____

5. Name the employees who live in Alexandria, VA.

_____

_____

_____

6. Name the employees who will be working at 5:15 P.M. on the first day of the restaurant's operation.

_____

_____

_____

7. What is the total pay for the five days worked by Jane T. Abbott?

7. _____

8. When did the employee with social security number 361-26-0916 clock out on the last day he or she worked?

8. _____

9. Create a query that lists the managers (e.g. manager, asst. manager, etc.). Use this query to make a report showing all the managers and their phone numbers. Print the report and attach it to this quiz.

10. Using the table showing employee information and the table showing workshift information, create a report that shows the time each employee is expected to begin and end his or her shift. The report should list the employee name, the date, and the start and end times of each employee's workshift. The report should be grouped by the date and should show information sorted by the beginning of the workshift. Print the report and attach it to this quiz.

# Student Notes

# Student Notes

# Student Notes

# Student Notes

# Student Notes

# Student Notes